"The Masculinity Workbook for Teens is the book adolescent boys and those of us who work with them have desperately wanted. Not because it has all the answers, but because it doesn't. It doesn't replace the 'guy code' with a set of more progressive rules. With respect and guidance, it empowers boys to explore and create their own guidelines for being a man. A magnificent achievement."

—**Stephen Tosh**, CEO of the Boys' Club of New York, career youth
worker, father of a son, and survivor of his own adolescence

"The Masculinity Workbook for Teens is an excellent resource for parents, caregivers, mentors, coaches, and educators to share with the boys in their lives. This practical guide empowers boys to navigate the 'guy code,' a set of unspoken rules they are pressured to follow to prove they are 'man enough.' Reigeluth has created an incredibly useful workbook for boys to do the inner work to uncover their whole humanity and authentic selves."

—**Jennifer Siebel Newsom**, filmmaker, and founder of
The Representation Project

"Young men long for us to acknowledge the realities of their lives; not to blame or shame them, nor condescend or lecture. What Christopher Reigeluth accomplishes so thoughtfully is to make this urgent conversation broadly accessible. By inviting boys to reflect on the air they breathe, he offers an invaluable guide to 'awakened masculinity.' I heartily recommend this workbook to all who care about boys."

—**Michael C. Reichert, PhD**, author of *How to Raise a Boy*, and
director of the Center for the Study of Boys' and Girls' Lives
at the University of Pennsylvania

"How do you talk to a boy about masculinity? About what it means to be a man? You can give your son this book, or you can use the personal stories, quotes, and exercises provided by Christopher Reigeluth to shape the conversations you'll have with your son over the next few years."

—**Andrew P. Smiler, PhD**, therapist, and author of the award-winning
Dating and Sex

"Teenage males probably would not ask for this book, but secretly I bet they all want this: an actual guide for being a man that goes beyond standard scripts and norms for how men are supposed to be. What makes this book wonderful is that it is more of a DIY guide to being the healthy and complete man that *you are* and want to be. All the young men in my life are getting copies."

—**Matt Englar-Carlson, PhD**, professor of counseling at California State
University, Fullerton; and director of the Center for Boys and Men

"*The Masculinity Workbook for Teens* is as important as it is timely. Timely because it identifies an underlying pathway to addressing the pain and confusion boys and men are feeling and perpetuating across America. Important because the workbook empowers and equips each reader to become part of the solution through the development and modeling of healthy masculinities."

> —**Joe Ehrmann**, author, activist, and president of the InSideOut Initiative—a national movement to reclaim the social-emotional and character development sports can and should provide for every participant

"This is the book that all people who care about boys have wanted for a very long time. It speaks *to* boys and not at them, and engages their natural intelligence and curiosity, including their ability to think critically and emotionally about their own experiences. The 'going deeper' sections are brilliantly constructed to get at what boys *really* think and feel, and not simply what they think they 'should' believe. The author even takes an intersectional approach in his discussion of identities, making it both a critically important book and a timely one. Buy it and give it to any boy or young man you know! You will change their lives."

> —**Niobe Way, EdD**, author of *Deep Secrets*—the inspiration for the Grand Prix-winning movie, *Close*, at the Cannes Film festival

"Boys need opportunities to explore who they want to be, not a society that imposes stereotypes dictating who boys should become. In this novel workbook for boys themselves, psychologist Chris Reigeluth offers a collection of distinct activities to help boys examine how the 'guy code' impairs their ability to choose who they want to become. School professionals and other concerned adults will find this workbook indispensable toward supporting boys' self-discovery."

> —**Joseph Derrick Nelson, PhD**, associate professor of educational studies at Swarthmore College, and senior research fellow with the Center for the Study of Boys' and Girls' Lives at the University of Pennsylvania

the masculinity workbook for teens

discover what being a guy means to you

CHRISTOPHER S. REIGELUTH, PhD

Instant Help Books
An Imprint of New Harbinger Publications, Inc.

Publisher's Note

INSTANT HELP, the Clock Logo, and NEW HARBINGER are trademarks of New Harbinger Publications, Inc.

New Harbinger Publications is an employee-owned company.

Instant Help Books
An imprint of New Harbinger Publications, Inc.
5674 Shattuck Avenue
Oakland, CA 94609
www.newharbinger.com

Cover design by Amy Shoup

Acquired by Georgia Kolias

Edited by James Lainsbury

Library of Congress Cataloging-in-Publication Data

Names: Reigeluth, Christopher S., author.

Title: The masculinity workbook for teens : discover what being a guy means to you / Christopher S. Reigeluth, PhD.

Description: Oakland, CA : Instant Help Books, [2022] | Includes bibliographical references. | Audience: Ages 13-19

Identifiers: LCCN 2022027973 | ISBN 9781684039494 (trade paperback)

Subjects: LCSH: Teenage boys--Psychology--Juvenile literature. | Masculinity--Juvenile literature. | BISAC: YOUNG ADULT NONFICTION / Boys & Men | YOUNG ADULT NONFICTION / Health & Daily Living / Maturing

Classification: LCC HQ797 .R46 2022 | DDC 155.5/32--dc23/eng/20220629

LC record available at https://lccn.loc.gov/2022027973

Printed in the United States of America

24   23   22

10   9   8   7   6   5   4   3   2   1   First Printing

To Finn (who will be a teen soon enough) and adolescent guys everywhere

Cracking the Guy Code to Be Your Authentic Self

Contents

Part 3: Who You Are and Your Awakened Masculinity

Foreword

When I was interviewing boys for *Raising Cain*, the book about the psychology of boys that Dan Kindlon and I wrote in 1999, I spoke at length with a ninth-grader about how boys manage those most human feelings of shame, sadness, and vulnerability. He acknowledged that most boys try to hide such feelings from others so that they won't look weak. We both knew that the desire to look strong is one of the requirements of masculinity that boys start to absorb by age three or four: "Boys are tough." "Boys don't cry." When I asked him what might happen if a boy kept his feelings to himself over a period of years, always trying to look more masculine, he observed, "Well, if you don't ever talk about them, you might not know what your feelings are."

Everyone who raises a boy, educates boys, or writes about boys worries about their emotional lives because we all see boys who cannot seem to recognize what they are truly feeling out of a desire to appear in charge, masculine, and tough. In the Academy Award–winning movie *Ordinary People*, a grief-stricken high school boy who has lost his brother in a boating accident goes to see a psychiatrist who asks him what he'd like to get out of therapy. The boy, who hasn't taken off his coat or his backpack and looks ready to bolt at any second, answers, "I want to be more in control." The psychiatrist, played brilliantly by the actor Judd Hirsch, recommends therapy twice a week. Immediately, the boy objects. The doctor explains, "Well, control is a tough nut." We recognize that he is slyly referring both to the impossibility of achieving perfect control in this life, but also describing the boy himself, who is going to be a very tough nut to crack. The boy is ready to endure months of strangulated pain and sadness rather than experience the helplessness and guilt—the weakness—of having been unable to save his brother's life.

Since I began speaking to parent audiences about boys, the number-one question I have had from mothers has been, "How do I get my son to talk to me?" When they are little, boys tend to be quite open with their moms, crying without embarrassment and reporting everything bad that happens to them. That continues up until around age nine. Then they start to fall silent or become more self-protective. Everyone who works with or loves adolescent boys knows that they can go deep inside themselves, presenting an outward picture of competence, even when their guts are churning and they are filled with doubt. A fourth-grade girl can come into her classroom on a Monday morning and tell her friends, "I hate my stepfather," and burst into tears. She will be surrounded by friends and encouraged to talk more. They will empathize and make suggestions. What about a fourth-grade boy who has experienced a terrible weekend with his stepfather? Can he cry to his friends and expect their support? No, he cannot. Why? He will have broken the rules that all boys know, and in so doing will make other boys uncomfortable. And if boys go for years without acknowledging their feelings, what happens to them?

Dan Kindlon and I called this phenomenon of the closed-down male adolescent who cannot identify his own feelings "emotional illiteracy." Others have called it the "mask" of masculinity. The makers of the film *The Mask You Live In* see boys "struggle to stay true to themselves while negotiating America's narrow definition of masculinity." Still others, like Bill Pollack, describe it as a "code" to which they must adhere. In this workbook for boys, Chris Reigeluth uses the term "Guy Code" (coined by Michael Kimmel). The Guy Code, he tells us, "is the set of rules that society…expects teen guys…to follow to meet expectations and be accepted." And follow them they do, often to their own detriment.

I return to my earlier observation: all of us who love boys or work with boys wish to free them from the constraints of a too-narrow definition of masculinity. However, by the time they are teenagers, they have internalized a lot of the requirements of a stereotyped masculine image, so physical strength, stoicism, silence, and risk taking, for example, are baked into them. Sadly, so are some really unattractive traits like arrogance, misogyny, and a willingness to prey sexually on women.

How successful are we in unwinding the powerful socialization of boys that goes on in peer groups (enforced by both boys and girls), in professional sports, in the media, in countless expressions of masculinity in the culture? Not very. We attack the most unattractive aspects of their masculine identities, we try to get under their armor, we try to coax them to embrace their "feminine side." When we—that is teachers, therapists, parents—tell boys that they are suffering from "toxic masculinity," they naturally react defensively. I have watched high school boys reject the efforts of teachers by dismissing them as "FemiNazis." (And don't even ask me about "androgyny workshops" for men back in the '70s. Oy!) When we ask boys too many emotion-laden questions, they often push us away. That is the painful experience of many mothers. When we preach to them about gender equity, they often get restless and bored. They typically see the need for gender equity when a girl they love is walking out the door. Experience does humble young men and change their understanding of true masculinity, but often too late.

Chris Reigeluth takes an innovative approach in this book. He offers boys a way to deconstruct the Guy Code on their own. He challenges them with a realistic assessment of what they are up against—every boy who reads his description of the Guy Code will recognize it immediately—and then he gets down to brass tacks. He describes real-life situations and gritty decision points. He offers boys choices, insight, and, most importantly, the chance to develop perspective in their own time.

In the last chapter of *Raising Cain*, entitled "What Boys Need," Dan and I wrote that we all should use boys as "consultants" on their own lives and as problem solvers. We also urged parents and educators to "teach boys that there are many ways to be a man." In this workbook, Chris does all of those things. He is constantly asking boys to solve intellectual problems; he is constantly asking them to reflect on their lives and choices. He touches on the highly visible elements of adolescent boy life, such as the use of "That's so gay," or the cruelty excused as "It's just joking," and then takes a boy to a deeper level by asking deeper questions: How does that feel? How do you react? Does that hurt? How do other boys understand these experiences?

I don't for a moment believe that a boy would casually pick up this workbook in a bookstore. (Do many teenage boys go into bookstores in person anymore?) That's not the relevant question for me. But if caregivers and mentors are able to get this valuable resource into the hands of the boys they love, those boys will have the opportunity to get to know themselves better as guys and people through this teen-friendly workbook. Furthermore, if a teacher introduced a group of boys to this workbook in a health class or in a course on gender identity, would the boys find it challenging, engaging, and informative? The answer is definitely yes. Does this workbook have the potential to change a boy's thinking about himself, his personal definition of masculinity, and how he relates to his friends? Yes, it does. Could this workbook help a boy to feel freed up emotionally, to be more accepting of his true self? Yes, it could.

Will all the boys who spend time with this book achieve what Chris calls an "awakened masculinity"? Perhaps not. But that's not the goal. The goal is to free boys; to have boys reflect on their identities, to think about the lives they are living and the impact they are going to have on others in the future. Chris Reigeluth is helping boys to develop the most important and precious ability that a human being can possess: self-knowledge.

—Michael G. Thompson, PhD
   Coauthor of *Raising Cain: Protecting the Emotional Life of Boys*

A Letter to Teen Guys

Hey!

I'm so glad you've picked up *The Masculinity Workbook for Teens* and are giving it a shot. I decided to write this because when I was your age there was a lot of pressure to fit in, prove oneself, and be "the man." This pressure could be pretty intense and sometimes made it hard to relax, even around my friends. Lots of guys were trying to outdo one another, and insults and teasing often flew around like pinballs. I know from talking with teen guys your age that there is still lots of pressure to fit in and prove yourself as a guy.

So, what is this constant teasing and pressure to prove ourselves as guys all about?

While I couldn't have answered this question at your age, I now know that the constant pressure many guys experience to prove that they belong and are "man enough" comes from something called the Guy Code (coined by Michael Kimmel, a sociologist). Have you heard of it, or do you have any guesses as to what it might be?

Simply put, the Guy Code is the set of rules that society—and consequently many of the boys, men, and other people you'll encounter—expects teen guys, like yourself, to follow to meet expectations and be accepted. We'll get into the actual rules soon enough, and you may even notice some of them jumping into your head as you read these sentences.

At your age, I knew exactly what was expected of me to be the "right" type of guy, and you probably do too. My friends and other guys also frequently reminded me of when I was failing to cut it. We all were! With few exceptions, it's pretty much impossible to be a teen boy and not have your friends or other guys give you a hard time about all sorts of stuff. The insults and pressure can be about anything, from something stupid you did to messing up at sports to wearing the wrong shirt.

What I didn't understand at the time is that I didn't have to buy into all of these masculinity expectations and the constant pressure to perform and prove myself. I didn't have to buy into society's narrow recipe for how guys should be, nor take it so seriously when other guys and people told me how I needed to be as "a guy." I had options and could decide for myself.

Now, I know what you're probably thinking: *Easier said than done, Chris.* Of course, you're right about that. The teenage years are no joke with social pressure and changes, like puberty, that can make everyone feel insecure and unsure about themselves. Furthermore, guys can be pretty hard on one another, and who wants to draw additional negative attention by going against the group and doing their own thing? Not many guys, that's for sure, including me when I was your age! So, we'll spend some time exploring the challenges of taking a stand, possible repercussions, and different ways to stand up for yourself and others (for if and when that's what feels right for you).

The other thing I didn't understand as a teen, and that we'll get into more, is that this Guy Code stuff isn't always so helpful, and it can have pretty negative consequences for guys. Now, that's not to say that it isn't working out just fine for you. You'll be able to assess the pros and cons of the Guy Code for yourself throughout this journey. Each of us is unique, and the ways that masculinity pressures impact each one of us will vary.

So, what am I getting at here? Well, I hope that all teen guys, like you, can be fully informed about what the Guy Code is, how it works, where it comes from, and, most importantly, how it influences them. With that understanding, you'll be able to more easily decide for yourself, and on your own terms, what type of guy and person you want to be.

Once you've made your way through *The Masculinity Workbook for Teens*, you might decide, *I'm good to go and not looking to make any changes.* Or, you might conclude that making a few small adjustments, or even big ones, is what feels right. There is no "correct" outcome or end result for this journey. My only agenda is to provide you (and other teen guys) with a greater understanding of how the Guy Code works and what it's all about, so you can be critical consumers and decide on your own terms who you are and how you want to be.

Let's get started!

Chris

Part 1

Getting Started

The Guy Code Is Everywhere, When You Know Where to Look

In case you missed it, please go back and check out "A Letter to Teen Guys," the book's opener. It's a good starting point and provides information on why I wrote *The Masculinity Workbook for Teens* and how I hope it will be useful for you.

Some Words on the Guy Code

When I was your age, I wish someone had given me a behind-the-scenes look at the pressures teen guys experience to prove themselves as being "manly." And that's what this book is all about—providing you with an insider's view of how this gender stuff works for guys, something most boys (and even men) don't get.

For my friends and me, and the other guys at my school and on my teams and in my clubs, we knew exactly what was expected of us as guys and of the importance of "being manly," which means the same thing as "masculine," another term you'll see in this book a lot. Those lessons and messages were crystal clear and started way before I became a teenager: "Suck it up," "Man up," "That looks _____," and "Don't be a _____." However, what we didn't get, and I certainly could have used, was someone sitting down with us to explain, "As guys, you're going to experience all of this pressure to be a certain way, and this is known as the 'Guy Code.' Some of these pressures and expectations might *feel just fine* and actually *be helpful*, whereas others *might not*. So, you've got some things to figure out for yourself, including what works for you and what doesn't."

Perhaps you've heard the term "Guy Code" (or something similar), or at least have a pretty clear sense of how society "expects" boys and men to be (whether you agree with all that or not). So, please take a moment to notice what comes up for you as you think about the different ways us guys are pressured by society and people to be a certain way.

The Guy Code (Kimmel 2008), also referred to as the "Boy Code" (Pollack 1998), is made up of the messages and rules that society gives us about *masculinity*:

- How to behave and act as guys

- What we should be good at and enjoy doing as guys

- How we are supposed to think and feel as guys

Another term that gets thrown around is "Bro Code" (Keith 2021). This represents more of an internal code of conduct for guys who identify as "bros" and includes stuff like "Guys come first," "Bros over hos," and "Don't get other guys into trouble."

While boys and men, including you and me, may have different thoughts and feelings about what it means to be a guy, a common thing we experience is pressure to prove our "masculinity" and "manhood" (Oransky and Fisher 2009). As teens we all pretty much encounter *pressure to*:

- Be tough

- Hide weaknesses and emotions

- Be great at sports

- Be in control and call the shots

- Be sexually interested in girls and women and hook up a lot

Have you experienced these types of pressures as a teen guy? Do others come to mind?

What You Can Expect

So, at this point you've heard a bit about why I wrote this book and how it might be useful for you. Now let me prepare you for what lies ahead.

All chapters include activities that will encourage you to reflect on your experiences as a guy, including times that Guy Code and masculinity pressures felt fine and helpful versus not so helpful. Some of these activities may feel comfortable and familiar, whereas others may take you into new territory and out of your comfort zone. Regardless, my hope is that you'll feel supported enough to think about this stuff for yourself and determine how you want to be as a guy, *which is up to you and you alone*. Most teen guys don't get invited to engage in this sort of self-exploration; I certainly wasn't. It just wasn't a thing people talked about or questioned when I was growing up.

The Masculinity Workbook for Teens consists of three parts. In part 1, which has already started to get into what the Guy Code is, I'll introduce key terms and you'll engage in gender-related activities, as well as explore how we learn about what's expected of us as guys. This part of the book is a bit terminology and concept heavy, and I apologize in advance, but please stick with it, because understanding these things will enable you to more fully understand how the Guy Code works and what it has meant for you so far. Part 2 focuses on the different Guy Code Rules and will invite you to personally investigate and more fully establish what kind of guy you want to be.

Finally, in part 3 you'll be able to put together the different things you've figured out about yourself during this journey and consider other important stuff, such as the cultural influences that are relevant to who you are as a guy and a person. While guys from all different backgrounds encounter similar pressures, such as to be tough, strong, and in control (Gilmore 1990), we can experience these pressures differently based on our unique identities, lives, and cultural backgrounds. The final chapter gives you space to further define *your own identity* as a guy.

This book includes several features that will support you as you explore masculinity pressures for yourself more deeply:

- **Words of Guys:** These sections offer short quotes from the experts, real teen guys of all different cultural backgrounds, reflecting on their experiences with the Guy Code and masculinity pressures. Unless otherwise cited, these quotes come from interviews I conducted with teens in middle school and high school and are appearing in print for the first time in this book. All names have been changed.

- **Stop and Think:** These sections offer questions for you to think about more deeply.

- **Research Moments:** In these sections I highlight information pulled from research on boys, men, and gender. (I also periodically provide *citations* that look like this: (Name Date). If you want to go deeper and learn more about a specific topic, you can find the source for each citation in the references at the back of the book.)

Throughout the book I share some of my own personal experiences and realizations, so you'll have a better sense of me and my journey. My experiences and the things I've learned *may or may not* resonate with you, which is totally fine. This is your journey for figuring out more about who you are and how you want to be, both as a guy and a person.

Covering the Basics

I was not educated on gender when I was your age. My friends and I were taught that there is *one way* to be a guy, and if you don't do what's expected then that will be a problem. Depending on the school you go to and what your parents or caregivers are like, perhaps you've been encouraged to think about what it means to be a guy, or perhaps your experience is similar to mine, and these topics haven't been introduced.

For example, I can remember taking a sex education class in the eighth grade with Mr. Baldwin, who actually did a pretty decent job. And yes, the class awkwardly included Mr. Baldwin showing us thirteen- and fourteen-year-old guys how condoms worked using a banana, which was hilarious and weird. Even though the class only had students in it who identified as guys, we were never taught about how the Guy Code works or encouraged to think about masculinity pressures for ourselves. Similarly, I don't remember any of my "wellness classes" in high school exploring gender stuff at all—almost like an unwritten rule exists that one's gender identity and society's expectations about masculinity shouldn't be questioned and explored. So that's exactly what we're going to do.

STOP AND THINK

How are you feeling about starting this journey? What sort of education have you received on gender and masculinity, if any, whether from caregivers, at school, or elsewhere?

ACTIVITY 1: Gender and Guy Code Self-Assessment

This first activity will help you check your understanding of gender basics. There's no expectation that you've been taught a lot, if anything, about these terms. I certainly hadn't been educated about the basics when I was your age. If you do know a lot about this stuff, then you're one of the fortunate ones. Understanding these gender basics will enable you to have a clearer sense of the different ways society teaches all of us guys what's expected, including how we are supposed to think and behave.

This self-assessment will serve as a baseline for your understanding of gender and masculinity pressures right now. Once you've worked your way through the book, it can be useful to return to this assessment and see where you started and reflect on where you're at now. Many readers will have experienced new realizations about themselves, such as how they define what being a guy means, and gained a fuller understanding of gender and the Guy Code.

Here goes, and no pressure. This certainly won't be graded and is just for you. Please fill in the blanks with your understanding of each term.

What's your understanding of the differences between "gender" and "sex"? (Keep in mind I'm not referring to sexual or reproductive activities.)

"Gender" is _____

_____.

"Sex" is _____

_____.

What's your understanding of the terms "masculinity" and "femininity"?

"Masculinity" refers to _____

_____

_____

_____.

"Femininity" refers to _____

_____

_____

_____.

Now, getting even more technical, have you heard the terms "gender binary" and "gender spectrum" (please circle one: Yes/No)? In general, "binary" means that there are two specific and clearly defined categories or parts, whereas "spectrum" includes a range of categories that are more open, fluid, and less clearly defined. So, with that in mind, please do your best to define these two terms.

Gender binary means: _____

_____

_____

Gender spectrum means: _____

_____

_____

Lastly, in the following box, please write in the different rules that come to mind when you think about the ways that guys are pressured to prove themselves and their manhood.

Guy Code Rules

Going Deeper

Nice work getting through the self-assessment. Now we're going to explore and unpack the stuff you were just asked about and make sure it makes sense. Let's start with *sex* and *gender*, two terms that many consider the starting point for any gender exploration. I certainly mixed these up when I was your age, and many adults do as well.

For all people, sex refers to the sex they are assigned at birth based on genitals and reproductive organs. Individuals born as the male sex type have a penis and testicles and typically more of the hormone testosterone, plus genetic material called "XY chromosomes." People born as the female sex type have a vulva and female reproductive organs, and typically more of the hormone estrogen, plus "XX chromosomes." While society typically focuses on male and female sex types, there are other sex categories, such as intersex, based on variations in people's genitals, chromosomes, and genes. When referring to a person's sex or sex type, the terms *male* and *female* frequently get used. (To learn more about any of these technical terms, you can do a quick Internet search or check out a biology textbook.)

In contrast, gender is frequently defined as the social behaviors and beliefs society expects of people based on the sex type they are born as (Kimmel 2016). Thus, in terms of the Guy Code, gender has to do with the behaviors and beliefs that society expects of boys and men, such as the:

- Clothing we're supposed to wear (for example, pants and T-shirts and preferably darker colors like blue)

- Activities we're expected to do and enjoy (for example, sports and video games)

- Ways we should be (for example, tough and not showing too much emotion)

So, based on being born with a penis and XY chromosomes, and belonging to the male sex type, boys and men are expected to behave and think in very specific ways.

The terms "male" and "female" are used to identify sex types, whereas "boy," "man," "girl," and "woman" are some of the terms that are used to refer to a person's gender. *Masculine* and *feminine* convey how much a person lives up to society's expectations (for example, "He's *soooo* masculine!"). To learn more about the differences between sex and gender, check out appendix A.

More and more, gender is being redefined. It's no longer uncommon for people to self-identify in ways that go against society's rules and expectations for boys, men, girls, and women (Gottlieb 2019). See appendix B for examples of additional gender identities that are more individualistic and less rule-bound.

Society's Gender Rules and the Boxes They Create

Let's shift gears a bit and look at the specific gender rules society has created and what that has meant for you. We'll now explore two more terms from the self-assessment, "gender binary" and "gender spectrum." I don't know about you, but as a teen I never heard these terms used.

As noted, something that is "binary" involves *two* things. Thus, "gender binary" refers to the traditional ways society has defined gender as being about two specific groups, boys/men and girls/women. While I never heard the term "gender binary" as a teen guy, I was well aware that society expected all people to fit themselves into one of two boxes: boy/man or girl/woman (Kivel 1992). A *limitation* of the gender binary that has achieved more acknowledgment of late is that plenty of people don't identify with either of these categories; they experience and express their gender uniquely and differently from what society expects.

The term *gender spectrum* encompasses the *full range* of diverse gender identities that exist. When I was growing up gender spectrum identities, such as gender-queer, pangender, and transgender, were not recognized or discussed. This may be the case for you, depending on where you live and who you hang out with. However, they are part of the gender spectrum that represents all different gender identities and expressions (see appendix B).

An underlying notion of the gender spectrum is that *gender is complicated*, and that our gender identities and expressions can shift throughout our lives. For example, as a teenager I didn't really question the ways society pressured me to be as a guy. Now, while I still identify as a guy, I more actively question the Guy Code and masculinity pressures, and I define what being a guy means to me more individually. How we express ourselves as guys can also shift from situation to situation. For instance, as a teenager I remember times when I felt like I really needed to "man up," such as at football practice, whereas in other situations, such as while hanging out with one of my best friends or my brother, I could relax and let my guard down more.

Does your community operate according to a gender binary worldview, or is there also support for people who identify on the gender spectrum? No judgment either way. How does your community's approach to gender feel for you?

In spite of there being a range of gender identities, many societies still frequently operate according to a gender binary outlook. Some examples of this include:

- Spaces that have girl and boy bathrooms but don't provide gender-neutral or nonbinary options

- Paperwork, forms, and surveys that only give *two* options for identifying one's gender

- The gender rules that exist for specific colors, such as blue being associated with boys/men and pink with girls/women. (When I was born, all babies went home from the hospital with a blue or pink blanket depending on their sex type. This type of gender binary color coding still happens at gender reveal parties for unborn babies.)

What other examples come to mind?

ACTIVITY 2: **The Gender Boxes**

In this exercise you'll consider "gender boxes" (Kivel 1992), society's expectations for how boys/ men and girls/women should think and behave (including the types of activities they should be into). So, the gender box for boys and men is equivalent to the Guy Code, whereas girls and women have their own gender box of rules—the Girl/Woman Code—they are expected to follow (Mahalik et al. 2005). Using two different colored pens (one for each gender category), please draw a line from each gender-specific descriptor (on the left) to the gender box you think it goes with based on society's rules and expectations.

Tough

Sensitive

Brave and risk taking

Athletic

Enjoys cooking

More academic/bookish

Caregiver/homemaker

Provider/bread winner

Strong and muscular

Stylish and fashionable

Emotionally expressive

Self-reliant

Player and stud

Dominant and powerful

Emotional control

Cooperative and nice

Thin body

More romantic

The answers can be found in appendix C. The more you got right, the more familiar you are with society's gender expectations and its rules for boys/men and girls/women, regardless of *whether you agree with them or not.*

Here are a few reflections from teen guys on what it means to "be a man" and the expectations teen guys experience.

Sammie, a twelfth-grader: That a man is somewhat stoic, caretaker, strong, independent, muscular, I guess. And I guess, like, those expectations of being manly and being a man should be the provider, courageous, yeah, I'd definitely say courageous and whatnot.

Jon, a first-year college student: Painless, fearless, um...do things on your own. You don't ask for help, really. Those kind of things. Those are the big ones... Also, something that comes to mind in terms of masculine—no feminine colors, yellows, baby blue, baby blue especially. Guys should wear more white, black, dark blue, dark greens.

Do you agree with Sammie's and Jon's reflections about what it means to "be a man"? Why or why not?

Going Deeper

Now that you've explored many of the differences between the societal expectations placed on boys and men versus girls and women, take a moment to consider whether you know of any boys or men *who don't always* follow the Guy Code rules. Because gender expectations are quite rigid and strict, it's pretty much impossible for any boy or man to *always* follow the rules and stay inside the box. That would literally require being a robot. Let's consider some of the ways boys and men can resist gender expectations (Way et al. 2014).

The following table offers examples of guys who challenge the Guy Code, known as "resisters," or those who go along with it, the "upholders." Consider whether you're more of a resister or an upholder in the given categories, and then provide an example of a way guys can resist masculinity expectations, whether you resist in this particular way or know someone who does.

Dress + Style	**Upholder:** Brad is pretty standard in his dress and generally wears blue jeans and T-shirts or flannels and really likes sports hats.
	Resister: Mel goes through periods of dying his hair different colors and sometimes wears nail polish.
Interests	**Upholder:** Like his older brothers, Arun plays lots of sports and doesn't put much effort into schoolwork.
	Resister: Justin plays sports, but he also sings in the choir, is really into language arts, and is one of the top students in his grade.
Emotional Expression	**Upholder:** Kenji doesn't show many feelings, besides anger, and even when feeling upset and down about things he keeps them to himself.
	Resister: Jesse is very emotionally expressive. Even though other guys tease him about it, he has cried at school and is more open with people about his emotions, like when he feels down.
Your Own Resister Example	

Gender Identity Is Up to You

So far, we've been exploring what gender is and digging into the different ways guys get pressured to prove their manhood and masculinity. Now it's time to ask what it all means for you, a question you'll be exploring throughout this journey. To put it another way, how have masculinity pressures impacted and influenced your life, including *what you're all about* and *how you feel about yourself* as a guy and as a person? This is a *big* question, I know, and we'll take it slow.

When considering this big question, it's helpful to take a look at your own gender identity. By the way, if as a teen someone had asked me, "What's your gender identity?" I would have initially felt a bit confused. Then I probably would have thought something like, *What is this person's deal?* and *No one has asked me that before.* And then, eventually, I would have responded with something like, "Well, I'm a guy, of course." I might have also just walked away from the person.

So, to recap, gender identity refers to how you internally experience and see yourself as a gendered person. While society typically approaches gender as binary and existing within the categories of boy/man and girl/woman, gender truly exists on a spectrum, and there are all sorts of different ways to identify and then express that identity to others. The gender category of "boy/man" can mean *lots* of different things to different guys:

- Many boys and men follow the Guy Code and society's expectations. How they experience themselves as a guy, and how they aspire to be, aligns pretty closely with society's masculinity blueprint (for example, being tough, strong, powerful, and into sports).

- Plenty of other boys and men identify with parts of the Guy Code, but not others. For example, as a teen toughness was definitely part of my identity and was very important to me. However, being a player and sexually active with lots of different girls was not really part of my internal identity (even though *I still pretended* to be all about that to fit in with other guys).

- Some guys reject all or most of the Guy Code and define what it means to be a guy on their own terms.

Which of these categories above rings truer for you? Your answer provides important information about your own gender identity and how you see yourself as a guy.

Along with your unique gender identity, which is internal, you also have ways that you visibly express that identity to others, called *gender expression*. Us guys can express our gender identity in different ways, such as with the clothing and types of shoes we wear, how we cut our hair, our music preferences, the activities we're into, and how we talk. The earlier examples of upholders and resisters highlight some of the different ways that guys can express their gender identity.

> *What comes to mind when you think about different guys you know and how they express what being a guy means to them, including yourself?*

Oh, yeah, it's really important to note that gender identity and expression for guys *don't always fully match up*. Sometimes we feel a certain way internally, but then express ourselves differently because we want to fit in and avoid being made fun of (as in my example of not personally identifying with being a player but acting like one in front of other guys to be accepted). Do you ever pretend in order to fit in?

ACTIVITY 3: My Gender Identity and Expression

Throughout this journey, I'll encourage you to think about your gender identity and expression. Please reflect on and answer the following questions.

What does being a guy mean to you (internally)?

_____

_____

_____

_____

How do you express this identity, such as through your choices in clothing, hair style, hobbies and activities, or anything else?

_____

_____

_____

_____

You'll have the chance to reflect on other parts of your identity and cultural background in chapter 8.

Words of Guys

As we've acknowledged, guys have all different ways of identifying what it means to "be a man," from traditional to more individual definitions.

Luis, a tenth-grader: I think being a man, just, from everything that I've learned, hmm, is to be the best that you can be. To always work your hardest. To not let obstacles stop you, and to always be there to give aid to people who need it, whether they're loved ones or strangers... Of course, I strongly, you know, have a belief that women should be able to do everything men can... I think a lot of people see being a man as having a nice girl or being some sort of a playboy or finding some way to make money.

Going Deeper

In reflecting on your gender identity (at this point in time), please circle "yes," "no," or "kind of" for whether each of the following masculinity pressures is a *part of your individual identity* as a guy, regardless of how you express these things externally.

- Always be tough   Yes | No | Kind of

- Don't cry or appear weak   Yes | No | Kind of

- Don't show your softer emotions, like sadness or worry   Yes | No | Kind of

- Be in control and in charge   Yes | No | Kind of

- Don't ask for help   Yes | No | Kind of

- Never back down   Yes | No | Kind of

- Excel at and dominate in athletics   Yes | No | Kind of

- Never act like "a girl"   Yes | No | Kind of

- Never act "gay"   Yes | No | Kind of

- Be sexually interested in girls/women and hook up a lot   Yes | No | Kind of

Hopefully this exercise offered you a chance to get to know yourself a little bit better. For any "kind of" responses, please give some thought to what makes those things less clear-cut than your "yes" or "no" responses.

Moving On

Great job getting through all that! I promise that future chapters won't be as terminology heavy. You now have a more solid foundation in gender basics to help you better understand how the Guy Code and masculinity pressures work. This foundation will ground you as you continue to explore for yourself *what you are all about* and *how you want to be*. You've also started to think more individually about what being a guy means to you and how you express that to others. It's not easy to do this work, and you're taking the steps and doing great. Onward!

Chapter 1

How We Learn About and Enforce the Guy Code

Alright, so at this point we've covered the more technical terms related to gender and the Guy Code. Hopefully it wasn't too painful. Now we'll go deeper and explore where the Guy Code comes from and how it makes its way to you. Most of us don't get invited to consider these important questions growing up, such as *Where do the pressures boys experience come from?* and *Why are there specific rules about how we're supposed to behave?* I certainly didn't. From talking with teen guys, as well as from reflecting on my own experience, I've concluded that the Guy Code is frequently just considered as "the way it's always been."

> **STOP AND THINK** *What's your sense of where the Guy Code actually comes from? If you haven't given this much thought, now is a great opportunity to do so.*

As a reminder, gender has traditionally been defined as the behaviors and beliefs that society expects of people based on their sex assigned at birth, most commonly male or female. Thus, our understanding of gender comes *directly from society*, in contrast to sex, which is biological and has to do with hormones, chromosomes, and genitals. Society educates people through a process called *socialization*, through which it imparts the rules and expectations of everything, from how we are expected to behave as guys to table manners to library etiquette. Getting even more precise, *masculine gender socialization* covers societal rules and masculinity teachings specific to us guys (Reigeluth, in press). Gender socialization happens in lots of ways for us, such as through:

- The toys we're given

- The type of clothing we're provided

- The shows we're encouraged and allowed to watch

- The messages we receive about the behaviors expected of guys

- The ways other boys and men act and behave themselves

An example of masculine gender socialization in action is the use of the phrase "Big boys don't cry." Whether you've heard that phrase directly or are just aware of it, it speaks for itself. "Big boys don't cry" clearly communicates the societal expectation that, in most situations, it's not acceptable for guys to cry or express *soft emotions* like sadness, worry, or fear. (More to come on the topic of emotions in the next chapter.)

Societies and their rules change with time. So, the expectations for guys today differ somewhat from those for older male caregivers and mentors, including dads, uncles, grandfathers, and other important men in our lives (just ask them).

When we're young, parents and caregivers often have the greatest influence when it comes to what we learn about gender and what it means to be a guy. I can remember looking up to all sorts of male mentors, including uncles, my dad, coaches, and certain teachers in both middle school and high school. After childhood, parents and caregivers no longer have the influence they did when you were a kid. From this point on, for most of us, other teenagers become the primary source of information about gender and what's expected of guys, including how to act and what we should be into.

ACTIVITY 4: Your Masculinity Education

Please identify two times (the earliest or most recent and the most memorable) when someone tried to influence your beliefs about what it means to "be a guy." Be sure to write down who the person is and how old they were, what they did or said to try to influence your behavior or beliefs, and how their message made you feel.

To get you started, here's an example:

Mohammed, a seventh-grader: Earlier this year, I remember wearing a sweatshirt to school that my aunt gave me. It had a rainbow on it. The guys let me hear about it as soon as I walked into school: "Nice gay shirt," and all sorts of other things. It didn't feel very good, but I laughed it off. I think some of the guys were kind of joking, but not really.

Earliest or most recent experience: _____

_____

_____

_____

_____

_____

Most memorable experience: _____

_____

_____

_____

_____

_____

Going Deeper

Please give some thought to the ways that your parents, caregivers, or other important people in your life have influenced your identity as a guy. For each of the following categories, circle "yes," "no," or "kind of" for whether they've raised you in traditional and more standard ways regarding gender and masculinity practices. Then, in each section, write down any examples you can think of. I included my own responses to provide some examples.

Toys   Yes | No | Kind of

For me, this is a "kind of." I remember being given and having fairly traditional toys for a boy, such as toy soldiers, G.I. Joes, and pocket knives, as well as books and stuffed animals. I answered "kind of" because my parents also got me into other stuff, like collecting sea glass at the beach and craft projects. I also don't ever remember being told I couldn't have something because it was "a girl toy."

Clothing   Yes | No | Kind of

That's a "yes" for me and I pretty much always dressed in or was given what is considered traditional boy clothing, like blue jeans, shorts, T-shirts, sneakers, collared shirts, sweatshirts, and baseball hats.

Room decorations   Yes | No | Kind of

For me, this is a "kind of." I don't remember my room being particularly "boyish" when I was younger. But, it certainly was in middle school and high school, with all of the sports and other types of "guy posters" on my walls. By that point, I was the one decorating my room, and my parents supported me in doing it how I wanted.

Messages about how you should be as a guy   Yes | No | Kind of

This is another "kind of." I don't remember receiving much verbal pressure from my immediate family to be a certain way. Every once in a while my dad used to make a joke that went something like "When men were men..." to jokingly convey that times had changed and guys weren't as tough as they once had been. It was funny and also reinforced societal expectations for how guys were expected to be. Some of my uncles were pretty intense with the masculinity pressure and insults.

The Most Important People Who Have Influenced You

Many of us don't think very much about masculinity pressures or who influenced or influences us. We also aren't encouraged to think critically about gender and what being a guy means. I certainly wasn't. Like breathing, society treats the Guy Code as automatic and a given, something not to be thought about or questioned.

Throughout our lives, and certainly during childhood and the teen years, we are all influenced by a variety of people, including other kids, caregivers, adult mentors, and famous people, who impact how we approach masculinity pressures and what we're all about as guys. They can directly influence our understanding of masculinity expectations with messages like "Suck it up" or "That's for girls," but we also learn about what's expected through *modeling*, which occurs when someone, typically a guy who is older, demonstrates how we're expected to be (Bandura 1977). These demonstrations can be about all sorts of different things, such as:

- How we're expected to dress and what colors are appropriate

- How we're expected to communicate and what topics are acceptable

- How we're expected to carry ourselves emotionally

- How we're expected to take an interest in certain things and not others

For example, while not aware of it at the time, I can now see how much influence some of my much older cousins had on me through masculinity modeling. At holiday gatherings, they carried themselves with lots of toughness and minimal emotional displays. They also wore "masculine clothing" of basic and darker colors and engaged in lots of joking, shit giving, and physical play, as well as heavy doses of sports talk. They were typically fun to hang out with and taught me about how guys are expected to think, act, and feel.

ACTIVITY 5: Personal and Famous Influencers

I invite you to take a moment to think about the important people in your everyday life who have taught you something about gender and have influenced your beliefs about masculinity, whatever they are. Perhaps there's an influencer who taught you to follow all of the Guy Code, certain parts of it, or none of it. Feel free to include people of different genders, as this is really about reflecting on the most important people to you, not just men.

Using the following spaces, please identify these individuals in whatever way feels comfortable to you, and write down how they've influenced your beliefs about gender and what being a guy means to you.

Personal influencer #1: _____

_____

_____

_____

_____

_____

Personal influencer #2: _____

_____

_____

_____

_____

_____

In addition to personal influencers, famous influencers, such as Hollywood stars, professional athletes, and even YouTubers, can be role models for teen boys. Depending on the star, they can either reinforce societal messages about manhood or challenge them.

On the following lines, please identify a famous influencer who is important to you, and write about how they've influenced your beliefs about gender and what being a guy means.

Famous influencer: _____

_____

_____

_____

_____

_____

When I was a teen, my famous influencers were primarily action heroes and sports stars who met societal ideals for how guys were expected to be and look (for example, big muscles, hardened and tough, and sexually active with women).

Due to society's influence, kids start to understand gender and the accompanying Guy and Girl/Woman Codes at a pretty young age (Martin, Ruble, and Szkrybalo 2002). Here are a few examples:

- By ages two to three, most toddlers recognize themselves as a boy or a girl.

- By ages four to five, most children can identify socially "appropriate" things for boys or girls, such as boys are expected to be into sports, play with trucks, and avoid things associated with girls like dress-up or playing with dolls.

- By kindergarten, boys can start to exclude girls from their play, along with boys accused of being "girlie" or insufficiently masculine (Chu 2014).

Going Deeper

Just as other people have served as influencers and role models for you, you will have the chance to influence the behaviors of others, especially guys who are younger. When you think about the type of role model you want to be, what words and descriptors come to mind? Different guys will respond to this differently. Here's an example to get you started:

Daisuke, a tenth-grader: Not sure and haven't really thought about that before. I guess I'd want to set an example, kind of—be someone who they look up to who does the right thing, is nice to other people, is good at sports, and also works hard at school. That's all I can think of right now.

I want to be the kind of role model for other guys who is: _____

_____

_____

_____

_____

Being a Guy Brings Lots of Pressure

I don't know about you, but when I was a teen I felt lots of pressure to perform and prove myself, especially around other guys. That's not to say that teens who identify with other genders don't also feel lots of pressure, because they certainly do. Guys experience unique pressures related to constantly having to prove ourselves to avoid being put down and losing status. Some of the more common pressures we experience include doing well at sports, not crying or appearing upset, being in control and in charge, and, as we get older, proving ourselves sexually with girls and women.

Guys also experience pressure around *social teasing* (Oransky and Fisher 2009); we're expected to be able to joke around and not take teasing too seriously. Boys who appear bothered by teasing, or fail to adequately respond with their own insults, can experience even more teasing and a loss of status. That definitely happened to me when I just couldn't come up with anything good in response.

Back-and-forth teasing, when done playfully, can certainly be fun. I remember lots of times when that was the case. Interestingly, for many guys, this form of interacting is also a way for us to connect when we're feeling bothered or down or dealing with difficult and sensitive stuff, because we experience so much pressure to avoid negative emotions and being vulnerable.

How do you and the guys you hang out with communicate? Have you ever been in a situation where a friend or another guy shared something personal and sensitive, and you didn't know how to respond? If so, what got in the way?

So, why do guys put so much pressure on one another to perform and constantly prove ourselves? Well, lots of this pressure is passed down to us from society and the constant expectation that, as guys, we need to prove that we belong and are good enough (or else). The trouble is the pressure doesn't really ever end, and there's always more proving to do right around the corner (Vandello et al. 2008). For many guys, all of this pressure can be pretty exhausting and even make it hard to relax around friends and other guys.

ACTIVITY 6: Pressure to Perform

Please circle "yes" or "no" to indicate whether you've encountered the following pressures that guys frequently experience. Feel free to add any examples I left out that are relevant for you on the blank lines. Also, please add a star to things you enjoy in spite of the pressures you've experienced to do them. For example, as a teen I experienced a lot of pressure to be good at sports, and I also naturally enjoy sports and continue to as an adult.

I've felt pressure to prove myself by...	
Wrestling or roughhousing	Yes | No
Playing sports well	Yes | No
Appearing disinterested in school/academics	Yes | No
Wearing a masculine style of clothing	Yes | No
"Hooking up" with girls	Yes | No
Not crying in public or openly	Yes | No
Not talking about my feelings	Yes | No

Not taking teasing too seriously	Yes | No
Making fun of other guys	Yes | No
Being into certain music or movies	Yes | No
Avoiding activities/items associated with girls	Yes | No
Taking risks or accepting dares	Yes | No
Not backing down from a fight	Yes | No
Being good at video games	Yes | No
	Yes | No
	Yes | No
	Yes | No

The number of responses you circled "yes" for provides an indication of how much pressure you've experienced to prove yourself as a guy. I would've circled "yes" for all of these as a teen.

Going Deeper

Have you considered the amount of pressure you feel to prove yourself as a guy in different settings? For instance, many guys experience more pressure to prove themselves in large groups of guys, and less pressure in smaller groups or when they're alone. Furthermore, certain spaces, such as locker rooms, can cause guys to feel more pressure, whereas the library may exert none.

Please read through the following examples of typical teen settings. Then consider whether the example is a setting where you experience more or less pressure to prove yourself as a guy, and place a checkmark in the appropriate column. Some settings may not apply to you, and it's fine to skip them. Feel free to write any additional relevant settings in the blank spaces. As you answer, please also consider what it is about the different settings that makes them more or less pressure-filled.

Teen Settings	Settings Where I Feel More Pressure	Settings Where I Feel Less Pressure
Sports practice		
Class		
Hanging out with just guys		
Hanging out with just girls		
At home		
Hanging out with friends of different genders		
Locker room		
By myself		
Hanging out with my close guy friends		
On the bus		
Recess or free time		
At parties		
Hanging out with my whole family		
Hanging out with just my dad or a male caregiver		
Hanging out with just my mom or a non-male caregiver		

Feeling pressure is inevitable in life; some of us feel more than others. However, if your responses above indicate a higher percentage of settings with *more pressure*, you may want to consider finding a way to get more balance, such as by identifying some new people to hang out with or taking on some new activities that allow you to relax and chill.

Policing of Masculinity and Me

There are many ways that we learn about the Guy Code, including *policing of masculinity* (POM), which occurs any time a boy or man receives the message that his behavior is not masculine enough, and that he's not living up to expectations (Frosh, Phoenix, and Pattman 2002). Essentially guys (and other people) can act like the "masculinity police" and let one another know when they're not meeting expectations and following "the rules." The most common way that guys engage in POM is through verbal insults, like "Man up," "Don't be a pussy/bitch," "That's so gay," and "Suck it up." While not as common, POM also occurs through physical aggression, roughhousing, and challenges and dares (Reigeluth and Addis 2021). What other examples can you think of?

I don't know how it's been for you, but I heard a lot of those insults growing up. They were frequently in the air, whether directed at me or other guys, and I dished them out too. Of my many experiences with POM, one that sticks in my mind occurred when I was in the eighth grade. I was excited to be in my first dating relationship, but also nervous. My friend Alan had more experience than me and was pressuring me to "make a move." When I didn't do so quickly enough by his standards, he called me "a prude," and some other guys chimed in with "scaredy-cat" and other insults. They did it in a joking way, but were also serious. It didn't feel great and made me even more nervous about this new thing, kissing, that I hadn't done before.

POM happens to us all growing up, even popular guys. When was the first time your masculinity was policed? What about the most recent time? Are there particular experiences that stand out, and if so, why?

POM messages can be intended as joking, to provide motivation, or to be mean. In all cases, POM communicates that *how you are being or performing right now is not good enough and not meeting expectations for how guys should be.* Even when it comes across as joking, POM leads many boys to change their behavior and act more masculine to avoid future put-downs. Guys can have their masculinity policed for all sorts of reasons:

- Seeming sad or bothered about something

- Not being good at sports or other "preferred" activities

- Wearing clothes or being into things perceived as unmasculine or feminine

- Being experienced by other guys as annoying or overly enthusiastic

- Being noticeably into school and academics

- Being less interested, or even disinterested, in girls sexually, or being deemed as unsuccessful in this realm (like me in the previous recollection)

What other examples come to mind?

Words of Guys

In coming to understand policing of masculinity better, the chief experts I've learned the most from are teen guys. Here are some reflections on why guys engage in POM. See if you have a similar or different take.

Bill, a twelfth-grader: If you did something wrong, then everyone will be like, "Oh, that's sissy that you did that... Oh, you can't do that. You must not be man enough to play football. You suck... You have a small dick." (Reigeluth and Addis 2016, 77)

José, a tenth-grader: I think [POM is], a lot of time, like a seesaw—like, bring one guy down, you seem a lot higher. So, a lot of the time, it's just to make certain guys make themselves seem manlier. So, we sort of balance each other out, keep each other at the same level. So whenever one guy gets dropped down, another guy gets brought up... When you're down, you just feel like the weakest of the group... And when you're up, you just feel like the alpha male. (Reigeluth and Addis 2016, 79)

ACTIVITY 7: "Come On, Be a Man"

Guys can have their masculinity policed for all different reasons, from obvious "masculinity violations" to seemingly random stuff. Here are some examples of teen guys' experiences with POM, including what happened (the situation), how the POM was dished out (the response), and the masculinity rule being enforced (the teaching). Please note whether you've experienced anything similar by writing in "yes," "no," or "kind of."

Situation (S)/Response (R)/Teaching (T)	Something Similar? (Yes/No/Kind of)
S: Adriel (a thirteen-year-old) tried to kick a soccer ball during gym and whiffed. R: Some other guys laughed and said, "Nice kick, girl." T: It's important to be good at sports.	
S: Max (a sixteen-year-old) was at summer camp and on a hike with a group of guys. He was struggling physically and falling behind. R: The counselor, Mike, shouted out, "Come on, suck it up. Let's go!" T: It's important to not struggle or show physical weakness.	
S: Jamal (an eighteen-year-old) went on a date and nothing physical happened. R: Afterward his guy friends asked how it went, and then jokingly called him "a prude" when he didn't say much. T: It's important to hook up and be sexually successful with girls and women.	
S: Amir (a fourteen-year-old) was hanging out with his older brother and some guys in the woods. They dared him to jump from one big rock to another about fifteen feet off the ground. R: When he responded with, "That's dumb; you do it," an older teen told him to "Man up" and then called him a "scaredy-cat." T: It's important to step up to challenges and dares and not show fear.	

Situation (S)/Response (R)/Teaching (T)	Something Similar? (Yes/No/ Kind of)
S: Burt (a fifteen-year-old) was quiet and dressed differently than most guys at his school. He was frequently teased and called names. One day he was in music class participating and singing enthusiastically. **R:** Tony, who frequently gave Burt a hard time, leaned forward, flicked his ear, and quietly said, "You're a fag." **T:** It's not okay to be different.	

For any "yes" or "kind of" responses, please take a moment to recall what those experiences felt like, which could have been anything from "No big deal" and "It was helpful" to "Really sucked" or "Felt bad."

In telling me about their experiences with POM, guys aged fourteen to nineteen talked about some of the different insults used to let other guys know their behavior isn't meeting expectations (Reigeluth and Addis 2016). Please circle any examples you're familiar with, whether you've had them directed at you, used them yourself, or heard another guy use them. Feel free to add in any additional insults I missed.

Fag	Pussy	Suck it up	Bros over hoes
That's so gay	Bitch	Toughen up	Wimp
No homo	Take off your skirt	Big boys don't cry	Whipped
Poofter		Man up	Small dick
Cocksucker	Girl		Skinny
Fruity	Girlie man		Shorty
	Sissy		
	Vagina		

Going Deeper

Guys have all sorts of emotional reactions to having their masculinity policed, from feeling like it's no big deal or funny to feeling bothered or hurt. Guys can also find it motivating for different reasons, including because it encourages them to ask someone out or to try harder in sports and other activities.

In thinking about the different ways that guys experience POM, how much of a problem do you think it is *for guys in general* (please circle one; adapted from Reigeluth and Addis 2021):

Not a problem   Sort of a problem   A major problem

Please clarify your answer in a few sentences: _____

_____

_____

_____

_____

In thinking about the different ways that you've experienced POM, how much of a problem is it *for you* (please circle one):

Not a problem   Sort of a problem   A major problem

Please clarify your answer in a few sentences: _____

_____

_____

_____

_____

Moving On

So that wraps up the basics of how we're taught about the Guy Code and masculinity expectations. In learning more about this stuff and how it all works, you're becoming more informed about gender and masculinity than most people—certainly more so than me when I was your age. That's pretty cool! In this chapter you reflected on different masculinity influences and teachers you've encountered, including the people within your household and the guys you hang out with. Through this exploration, you took some big steps to better understand where the Guy Code comes from and the ways that masculinity pressures have influenced you. As we move on to part 2, we'll dig deeper into the specific Guy Code Rules and think more about how they've worked for you and, most importantly, how you want to be as a guy. Here we go!

How to Be a Guy...
You Decide

Chapter 2

Rule Number One

Guys Should Hide Difficult Emotions

As guys, we pretty much all receive the message that crying and "being emotional" are bad news. This starts early, as young as ages three and four, when we may literally be told, "Big boys don't cry," or something similar. By the time guys become teens, the message is the same, but now we're hearing things like "Suck it up," "Don't be a bitch," and so on. The emotions we are told to *avoid* the most include sadness, fear, doubt, insecurity, and disappointment (Oransky and Marecek 2009). Of course, there are exceptions to this pressure; for example, it's "acceptable" to see grown men crying after winning a sports championship or at funerals, or to see fathers get teary-eyed at major events for their kids. Regardless, the message to boys and men is generally clear: keep difficult emotions to yourself.

 When do you think it's acceptable for guys your age to show difficult emotions, and when have you seen other teen guys be vulnerable—that is, let others know they're feeling hurt or struggling?

So, let me be up-front about the bind this rule places upon us guys. From a young age, we all receive these messages telling us to steer clear of vulnerable emotions, but, in actuality, all guys experience these softer emotions, including sadness, fear, and worry. To never feel upset or insecure you'd have to be a robot, because experiencing *all* emotions, including the vulnerable ones, is what makes us human.

I don't know about you, but I can remember times in middle school and high school when I let a few tears sneak out or showed other guys that something bothered me. For instance, in ninth grade I remember this kid kept calling me out for being "skinny," along with other things. He just wouldn't let it go, and then other guys would laugh and chime in, making it worse. While I had pretty clearly committed to heart the rule "Big boys don't cry," which also just means "Don't show other guys you're feeling bothered," I got pretty upset, and the name-calling just increased.

What was the end result of all this, you might wonder? Well, as a teen, I had fully bought into the Guy Code, so these types of callouts led to me feeling not good enough, keeping more things to myself, and trying harder to hide difficult feelings, like worry and sadness, to avoid being put down. With time, I got pretty good at keeping tough stuff and vulnerable emotions to myself and not showing them to others, including my parents. My sense is lots of guys struggle with letting others know when they're going through tough times for fear of getting made fun of.

Can you remember any times when you got emotional in front of other guys or showed them you were upset? What happened and how did you feel afterward?

While this rule applies to the more difficult and softer emotions, like sadness, worry, and fear, it straight-up doesn't apply to emotions that don't express vulnerability, like anger, frustration, hostility, and resentment. Sure, as you've likely witnessed, guys can get teased when they lose control of their anger, "spaz out," and take things too far. But for the most part, society is more accepting of guys expressing these tougher, nonvulnerable emotions. Why might that be? Well, the "Don't mess with me" emotions line up perfectly with the Guy Code and can be used to gain control and power over others. They also provide a warning, such as "You're making me upset and angry and should stop, or there will be consequences."

So, why do guys experience pressure to hide vulnerable emotions, and where does this rule come from? A big part of the answer relates to gaining and retaining power. Going back centuries, and even to ancient civilizations, men, whether they're kings, presidents, bosses, CEOs, or community leaders, have had the most control and influence over society. A system in which men have the most control and make the rules is called a *patriarchy* (Kimmel and Ferber 2017). While many societies have changed a lot, and continue to change in this regard, around the globe men continue to have more power and privilege than other groups (and white boys and men even more so). Part of staying in power is convincing others that you aren't weak or easily shaken. Vulnerable emotions, along with crying, are frequently viewed as a sign of weakness, even though we all experience them.

You may be guessing that I think it's important and healthy for guys to have ways to be vulnerable and express the tough stuff that's going on for them. Well, I do. I also recognize that there are times, for all of us, when we need to keep difficult emotions in check, sometimes for survival purposes, such as to avoid getting ripped on, and at other times to get through something rough, like a challenging day at school. This emotion stuff is complicated, and it's up to you to figure out what works best for you.

ACTIVITY 8: Learning to Hide Emotions

Regardless of whether you agree with this rule or not, or fall somewhere in the middle, all guys receive the message that it's important to hide vulnerable emotions. For this activity, take some time to think back on your life and the different experiences you've had when receiving the message that guys should keep difficult feelings to themselves. Then, in writing, please reflect on your earliest memory and the biggest-deal memory of this happening, including how old you were, what happened, and what the experience felt like.

Here is a sample response:

Xander, an eleventh-grader: Last year, I remember struggling because my girlfriend broke up with me. I was feeling super low and didn't even want to go to school or leave my house. I tried to talk to some of my friends about it and mentioned that I was "feeling pretty shitty." The responses I got were basically, "Move on," "You'll get over her," and "There'll be plenty of others." It felt crappy to be told that when I didn't feel like I could just move on.

Earliest memory: _____

_____

_____

_____

_____

_____

Biggest-deal memory: _____

_____

_____

_____

_____

_____

Tyrell, an eleventh-grader: You gotta be tough. You just got to, like, be strong. You have to hold your own ground, and you can't really show too much emotions. Like, I feel if people are close to you, yeah, show emotion. But, like, I feel in today's society, if you cry in front of a whole bunch of people, they're going to be like, "Oh, you're weak" or "You're not as manly as the next person." Like, if you see most of us guys, some of us don't like to talk about our problems. But then some do. Like, I know I'm not going to go out and discuss all of my problems and stuff like that. I'm just going to deal with them on my own. I feel, like, we're supposed to be more independent in doing what we need to do. And we have to be more men, and we have to act more mature at an early age.

Do you agree or disagree with Tyrell's comments about this Guy Code Rule? Why?

Going Deeper

It's easy to identify many of the ways that society communicates to us guys that difficult emotions are bad and should remain hidden. For instance:

- The phrase "Big boys don't cry" speaks for itself.

- When delivered in response to a guy having a tough time, the meaning behind insults like "Suck it up," "Man up," "Don't be a pussy," and "That's so gay" are crystal clear.

In the following box, please write down any insults you can think of that people have said to you directly or to other guys to enforce the rule that boys and men should keep difficult emotions to themselves. Next, circle any that you yourself have said to other guys. Guys are taught to say these things to one another, so most readers will be doing some circling, including myself.

Insults Said to Guys

Most guys who use insults like these will have gone "too far" at some point, such as by unintentionally hurting another guy's feelings. Have you done that, and if so, what happened and how did you respond?

All Emotions Are Important

Like gender, emotions also exist on a spectrum. On one end are the vulnerable and soft emotions, and on the other end are the "Don't mess with me" emotions. To be our best, all humans, including us guys, must be able to access the full range of our emotions and have ways to safely express them. Why is that, you may ask?

Well, emotions provide helpful bits of information about how we're doing at any one moment and how to respond to various situations. They also help us get to know ourselves better. For example, sadness conveys that we're feeling hurt or a sense of loss, like after an important relationship abruptly ends. It also lets us know that we need to take extra care of ourselves so we can recover. Anger, however, can signal that someone has wronged us, perhaps by spreading a rumor, and that it's important for us to get away from that person or to take a stand.

 What's your internal world like? Do you feel in touch with and open to what's going on emotionally, or are you frequently confused by or resistant to your different emotional states—or maybe both?

Our emotions are complicated and can shift quickly. We cycle through times of feeling "all good" to feeling like life couldn't suck any more to a mix of somewhere in between. Please mark an X below to indicate what your internal world has been like for the past week.

More Vulnerable   Mix of Both   More "Don't Mess
Emotions   with Me" Emotions

ACTIVITY 9: **Keeping It Real**

Because society is more approving of guys expressing "Don't mess with me" emotions, such as anger, many of us get a lot of practice reacting to threats and disappointment with aggression, and significantly less practice expressing softer and more vulnerable emotions, like sadness. With less practice, our emotion skills get rusty. I remember expressing anger lots of times in middle school and high school, when in reality I was feeling nervous or worried about something that was bothering me, like:

- *What will high school be like?*

- *Will I make the soccer team or some other team?*

- *Does my crush like me?*

- *Zits! Ughhh.*

- *Will I get into college?*

In the following exercise, please write down three things that bothered you in the past (or are bothering you now), that brought up vulnerable emotions, and that you shared with someone else (either through telling or showing). Please include how you shared the difficult thing and the outcome—that is, what happened. Outcomes from sharing with someone could include things like "Felt better," "Didn't feel better," "Friend supported me," "Friend wasn't helpful," and so on. To get you started, I included an example from Luca, a ninth-grader.

Stuff That Gets Me Down	How You Shared	Outcome
When my older brother is an asshole and says mean stuff.	My cousin could tell I was sad, and I let him know about this shitty thing my brother did to me.	He was cool about it. He also has an older brother and told me about stuff too.

Stuff That Gets Me Down	How You Shared	Outcome

Going Deeper

Emotional intelligence—being aware of all our different emotions and being able to express and communicate them to others—is very important for our well-being (Brackett, Rivers, and Salovey 2011; Kennedy-Moore and Watson 2001). Some benefits of emotional intelligence include:

- Stress reduction

- Improvement in your ability to handle complicated situations

- Increased speed with identifying dangers and threats

- Feeling more connected to friends and family

- Knowing yourself better

Please circle any of the benefits from the list above that you've experienced personally (during times when you're more aware of difficult emotions going on for you and are able to communicate about them with others). For any benefits you circled, also reflect on and notice any specific examples that come to mind. For example, when I'm worried about something, talking to my wife and close friends about the issue reduces my stress, and then I end up feeling more connected to them.

Words of Guys

Michael, a tenth-grader: The image of guys is tough and emotionless, but that subject's come up before, and I just come straight out: "I'm not afraid to cry." I'm not afraid to show emotions either, and it's really nothing bad. I mean, I'm tough, but I'm not afraid to cry. So, if a guy wants to think I'm afraid or a wuss because I cried, then let them think that. But if they want to fight me, "Let's go!"

Howie, a tenth-grader: When a guy shows emotions, that's when kids talk at them and call them "a fag" or "a pussy." Like if a guy shows that he's sad, and he cries or something, guys will call it, "Oh, so you're a pussy. You're crying. Only girls cry." And I don't see why that is because all girls could easily say guys get pissed off all the time, when they really don't. Because most guys that I know in school go home and cry. But they won't cry in front of their friends because they are afraid of being called "a pussy" or "a fag."

Do you agree with Michael that guys can be emotional and still be tough? Why or why not? Howie calls out "most guys" for fronting and being different in front of their friends than when they're alone. Is he right?

Sometimes You Gotta Keep Stuff to Yourself

No one can always be an open book with their emotions. Just as there are times when it's important to have trusted people in our corners, there are also times when we need to keep tough and sensitive stuff to ourselves, right? That's just reality, because some guys and other people can be pretty mean and harsh if you let your guard down at the wrong time. I can remember some older and bigger guys teasing me on the bus and cracking "yo' momma jokes" when I was in the fifth grade. It was bad enough that I couldn't get away, and it became even worse when I started to cry, which (big surprise) led to even more teasing.

STOP AND THINK

Have guys ever given you a hard time or been mean after you revealed vulnerable emotions? If so, what comes to mind?

Teen guys experience all sorts of rough situations that bring up difficult feelings, including:

- Being cut from a sports team, club, or other activity

- Challenges with friends

- Struggling academically

- Being pressured to get a job or go to college

- Getting dumped

- Family difficulties at home

Which of the above can you relate to? What other tough situations come to mind that are relevant to you and other teen guys?

Unfortunately, as you and I know, it's not always convenient, possible, or safe for us to stop what we're doing to process and make room for difficult emotions. There are plenty of times when teen guys need to keep vulnerable feelings to themselves to avoid teasing, or worse. In other moments, you might be dealing with something that needs immediate attention, like getting through the school day, practice, or finishing up at work.

STOP AND THINK *Have there been times when you had to keep difficult feelings to yourself to get through something or to avoid negative consequences? What was that like?*

So, just as emotional awareness and expression are skills, managing difficult feelings and keeping them to yourself (when necessary) are also skills.

ACTIVITY 10: Conceal or Reveal

In the three following scenarios, a teen boy encounters a difficult situation and is faced with the decision to conceal or reveal vulnerable emotions. Your task is to simply take in each scenario, and then think through how you might approach it (or something similar) and whether you would *conceal* or *reveal* your emotions.

A tenth-grader, Ivan, was recently cut from the varsity soccer team. He has played soccer for most of his life, including at summer soccer camps. He is worried that his parents will be disappointed and is feeling shame and embarrassment for not making the team after putting in such a big effort. His best friend Jason made the team, which makes it even worse. After a few days, Ivan finally lets his parents know what happened. When they ask how he is feeling, he responds, "It's no big deal. I don't like soccer that much anyway."

A twelfth-grader, Ryo, got blindsided when he found out that his boyfriend had been cheating on him. They had been dating for eight months. It was Ryo's longest relationship, and he feels "shattered." It's now been a week, and Ryo is still struggling to tell his friends how heartbroken he feels, and he doesn't want to be judged. Finally, he lets his close friend Will know, and Ryo feels supported.

Mitch, a seventh-grader, is hanging out with a group of guys from his middle school. He knows some of these guys pretty well and is less close with others. Mitch is feeling bummed because he recently learned that his mom lost her job. He's worried about his family and how they will get by. Mitch is debating whether to tell these guys about what's going on and how he's feeling.

Words of Guys

When going through tough times, friends can be really supportive, but, for some teen guys, they can also be pretty harsh.

Dominick, a tenth-grader: It was about a year ago. I was just, like, depressed all the time. And my friend called me "a depressed little bitch." And it really got to me because I had just lost my grandfather... When he said that to me, I learned to hide how I was feeling. I would put on a fake smile. (Reigeluth and Addis 2016, 80)

What are your friends like? Do you trust them enough to share sensitive stuff with them?

Going Deeper

It's important to have people with whom you can keep it real, can let your guard down, and don't have to perform. We all need these things; it's how we connect with others, develop meaningful relationships, and feel supported. I don't know how it is for you, but I definitely feel closest to the guys whom I can pretty much talk to about anything, including stuff that gets me down. These closer friends also share sensitive stuff with me. When guys don't have deep friendships like this, they can end up feeling alone, less supported, and like no one truly gets them.

Do you have someone whom you can share difficult things with and who supports you during tough times? For this short exercise, describe this person (or more than one). What about them helps you feel comfortable revealing more of yourself, whether you're having a good or a bad day? To get you started, I included a response from Robbie, an eighth-grader.

Person	What Are They Like?	How Do They Support You?
My friend Jeremy	He's cool and fun. We're the same age, and he lives next door. We hang out lots and like the same stuff.	Well, I can talk to Jeremy about stuff I can't with other people, like things about my family and that I worry about.

If this was a difficult exercise to complete, it will be important for you to work on developing relationships with guys and other people whom you can trust and be more real with. That might mean making new friends, which is never an easy thing to do but can be worth the effort.

When Hiding Emotions Goes Too Far

You may be asking yourself, *What's the big deal with hiding difficult emotions?* or feeling like *That's just the way it is.* I hear that and understand where you're coming from. When I was your age, I definitely didn't question or even consider the pressures guys experience to hide vulnerable emotions, and the pros and cons of doing so. No one taught me about this stuff.

For all people, there are definitely times when it's necessary to keep difficult feelings to oneself. This can be to avoid getting teased or bullied, to get through a tough day, or simply because you have other things going on that need your attention. But some guys can take hiding emotions too far, feeling like they have to be in control of them at *all* times, which often leads to problems.

> **STOP AND THINK** *Have you ever felt crappy when you didn't share something difficult that was going on for you? I certainly have. What comes to mind?*

ACTIVITY 11: Problems Can Arise

When guys keep difficult emotions bottled up and they don't have friends or other people to confide in, issues can arise (Kindlon and Thompson 1999; Way 2011). You may have experienced these issues directly, or know other guys who have struggled in the following ways. Most guys will have experienced some of these challenges at different times, including myself, even as an adult.

For each example, please place an *X* in the box if you have experienced the issue, and a circle if you know other guys who have. For some of the examples, there may be both an *X* and a circle.

 Feeling alone and like people close to you don't fully get you because you're keeping lots to yourself

 Feeling less connected to friends, or men in your life, because they don't share more openly

 When difficult emotions arise, you quickly push them down, which can lead you to not know yourself as well (for example, feeling constantly bothered or on edge and not sure why)

 Experiencing ongoing sadness or worry because you aren't dealing with or expressing the emotions you're pushing away

Getting angry more easily and having a short fuse, which frequently happens when you keep things that bother you to yourself

 Abusing substances or engaging in other risky behaviors, like fighting, as a way to deal with difficult feelings and stress

If you think of additional examples of ways this pressure to hide emotions can create problems, whether for yourself or others, please write them here:

_____

_____

_____

_____

While the above challenges are no fun, you can work to address them by finding people you trust, and then taking steps to share more openly when you're experiencing tough stuff.

 Research Moment Research indicates that younger boys are more emotionally vulnerable with their friends and use words like "love" and "happy" when describing friendships (Way 2011). As boys get closer to high school age and experience pressure to hide emotions, their language can start to include more expressions of anger, frustration, and lack of caring, which leads to friendships that are less close. As you've gotten older, have you experienced anything like this in any of your friendships with guys?

Going Deeper

Do you know any guys who have a difficult time being vulnerable or sharing what's going on for them, or who seem kind of withdrawn and rarely smile? For some of us, our examples could be our dad or a caregiver, an uncle, a friend, or an older brother. Please use the following spaces to describe someone who seems to fully buy into the pressures to keep difficult emotions to themselves.

How can you tell that they take this Guy Code Rule so seriously?

_____

_____

_____

How does this person's difficulty being more real and open impact your relationship, and what, if anything, do you wish could be different?

_____

_____

_____

_____

_____

With regard to this guy you know, please consider whether it would be worth saying anything to him about your observations and the things you wish could be different.

What's Your Take?

Okay, you've now had the chance to think a lot about Guy Code Rule Number One and hopefully understand it in some new ways, especially as it relates to you. So, let's see where you stand with it.

ACTIVITY 12: Rule Number One and You

At this point in the journey, do you think that hiding vulnerable emotions is an issue for you or other guys? Why or why not? Use the space below to reflect on your feelings about this rule.

- In particular, consider how this rule has worked for you and how you want to be.

- If you have mixed feelings, please identify the pros and cons of following this rule for you and other guys.

_____

_____

_____

_____

_____

_____

_____

_____

_____

_____

Moving On

So that sums up our exploration of Rule Number One. Most guys don't get invited to explore the ways society pressures them to keep vulnerable and more complicated feelings to themselves. They also aren't told about the consequences for boys and men who take this Guy Code Rule to the extreme and don't have people with whom they can be more real. Nice work sticking with some challenging topics and putting yourself out there. You've now cracked the code on this rule, which hopefully puts you in a better position to decide how you want to be as a guy. Keep it up!

Chapter 3

Rule Number Two

Guys Should Be Tough at All Times

I don't know how it's been for you, but when I was a teen I remember feeling lots of pressure from other guys to prove my toughness. As guys, we receive all sorts of messages about the importance of being tough, such as through the use of common and unmistakable phrases like "Man up" and "Suck it up." While some guys are pressured or put down more than others, no guy is immune from these types of insults, including myself—even when I was in college.

> **STOP AND THINK** *What do phrases like "Man up" or "Suck it up" mean to you? Do any specific times come to mind of when you heard, or used, phrases like "Man up" or "Suck it up"? If so, what were those experiences like?*

As we know, these types of insults, or "fronts," can be said in a joking way, like when friends are playing around, or in a harsh way, such as to make another guy feel super low. Interestingly, whether guys (or anyone, for that matter) intend to be joking or mean, any time a phrase like "Man up," "Suck it up," "Grow some balls," or something similar is used, it reminds other guys that they're expected to be tough, to be fearless, and to feel no pain.

Words of Guys

Marco, a tenth-grader: I guess it would be more of how to test one another and see if you're, like, able to join or be acceptable in this wolf pack...to be a male in society's eye per se, to be tough and masculine, to not be a little bitch, to [not] be afraid to do things, to be the bigger man. (Reigeluth and Addis 2016, 78)

Do you agree with Marco's description of the ways guys are expected to be tough, which includes not being afraid? What other ways come to mind? What's your understanding of the "wolf pack"?

So, where does this rule—to be tough at all times—come from, and why do guys feel pressure to adhere to it? Well, as we'll explore, demonstrating toughness (which often includes taking risks) is a key way that many guys try to prove their superiority to other guys, while at the same time distancing themselves from anything considered "feminine" or "gay." (Much more to come on these topics in chapter 7.)

There are times for all people, including guys, when toughness helps us accomplish something big, like winning an Olympic medal or responding to a crisis. Life can be challenging, and toughness and risk taking are essential ingredients for success.

For instance, I was really into hiking and camping with friends when I was a teenager. I can remember getting stuck in awful weather, including having to hunker down beneath trees while lightning flashed overhead. Uncomfortable and sometimes scary moments like these required mental and physical toughness. And getting through these challenges with friends led to us feeling closer afterward. Pretty cool. Have you and your friends gotten through scary moments and challenges together? If so, did you feel closer afterward?

So, if all people can benefit from having the ability to be tough, why are the pressures that teen guys experience unique? Well, many boys, including me when I was your age, experience constant and intense pressure to prove themselves (Levant et al. 2012). As you know, guys are expected to be tough in all sorts of different ways, such as by:

- Playing sports physically (for example, taking or offering a big hit) and not cracking under pressure

- Not letting others know you're in pain or are upset if you get hurt, either physically or emotionally (such as by being dumped)

- Not backing down if another guy disses or challenges you (including to fight)

- Not complaining about or seeming bothered by anything

My friends and I even pressured each other by "playing" games meant to test one another's toughness, such as "Butt's Up," "Bloody Knuckles," and "Slaps." What all of these games have in common is the requirement to prove one's toughness by demonstrating a pain tolerance, sometimes at pretty significant levels, by having your knuckles smashed, hands slapped, and so forth—hard. Have you and your friends ever played these types of games? If so, what do you think of them?

While lots of guys have shared with me how they think the pressure to be tough, including taking risks, can help motivate them to achieve more, they've also reflected on when it goes too far, like when a guy gets put in a dangerous situation or does something he really doesn't want to do. So, let's take a closer look at both the pros and the cons of the pressure to be tough.

ACTIVITY 13: "Man Up" Memories

Please identify two times when you learned about the importance of toughness for guys. Perhaps you were told directly to "Man up" or "Suck it up," or perhaps you learned in some other way. Include a memory from when you were younger, and something more recent, but, most importantly, pick moments that stand out in your mind. Be sure to include what the person said or did to let you know that you needed to toughen up, and how their message made you feel (for example, "Didn't like it," "Felt shitty," "Not a big deal," or "Felt fine and was just what I needed").

To help get you started, here's an example from Pedro, a sixteen-year-old tenth-grader, who told me about his drill sergeant calling him a "girl":

I felt bad in the beginning. But, as a couple minutes went by, when I was just, like, holding myself up there, I was like, You know what? He's right. Just toughen up... Basically just toughen up if you're cold. Suck it up. If you get a cut, don't go to the nurse. I'm not going to complain for any little thing. (Reigeluth and Addis 2016, 80)

Your example #1: _____

_____

_____

_____

_____

Your example #2: _____

_____

_____

_____

_____

Going Deeper

Guys are pressured to be tough in all sorts of different ways. Sometimes this pressure can be helpful, such as when you need to get through something difficult, and sometimes it can be hurtful, such as when the pressure feels like too much or you feel like you don't have a choice in the matter. Take a moment to answer the following prompts, writing about times when the pressure to be tough felt helpful versus harmful.

A time when the pressure to be tough felt helpful: _____

_____

_____

This experience felt helpful because _____

_____.

A time when the pressure to be tough felt harmful: _____

_____

_____

This experience felt harmful because _____

_____.

Toughness and You

Now, let's turn our attention to what toughness has meant to you in your life. Pretty much all of us know how the Guy Code defines "toughness," right? When I was your age, my version of toughness aligned with the Guy Code. Thus, I was taught and believed that "toughness" means *never* backing down from a challenge and showing no weakness, fear, or pain.

We don't often get asked what "toughness" means for us individually. So, what's your take on what it means to be tough? Do you define "toughness" as I did—and many other guys do—when I was a teenager, or do you have a different definition?

At this point in my life, I define "toughness" differently from my teenage self. With time, and enough things not working out so well due to feeling like I had to be tough all the time, I've come to realize that it's okay to say no to dares and challenges, such as being pressured to chug a beer or do something that might hurt or get me into trouble. But that's just me, and it's taken a lot of life experience, experimenting, and regrets to get me to the understanding that I *don't always* have to be tough. It will be helpful to figure out for yourself what "toughness" means for you, and what you're all about.

I'm aware of and remember well the social pressures teen guys face, including the constant threat of getting teased or shown up. It's not easy to say no, and doing so can quickly lead to you getting called out or receiving more group pressure, neither of which are fun. So, later in the chapter I'll share tips and strategies for saying no.

Like lots of guys, you may feel like it's really important to be tough and to demonstrate toughness to others as much as possible, or you may feel differently. To help you understand yourself a bit better, take a moment to consider *how much pressure you put on yourself* to be tough in front of other guys. Please mark an X below for the level of pressure that best represents you.

No Pressure at All	Some Pressure	Lots of Pressure

In general, how has this level of pressure worked for you?

- For instance, if you put "lots of pressure" on yourself to be tough, has that contributed to you feeling more fulfilled and happy as a person? Has this pressure ever felt like too much or led to bad outcomes?

- Or, if you put "no pressure at all" on yourself, how has that felt? Have you experienced situations when exerting more toughness could have been helpful?

Research Moment

Media—such as movies, video games, and TV shows—can exert pressure on boys and men to be tough and take risks. Boys and men are frequently portrayed in unrealistic ways that include humongous muscles, hyperaggressive and violent activities, and constant risk taking (Smiler 2019). These portrayals have shifted quite a bit in the last sixty-plus years. You can quickly assess this change yourself, if you want; Google "Superman of the 1950s and 1960s," or Batman, and compare the images that pop up to those of the 2000s onward. You'll notice a pretty big difference in how these superheroes are presented these days: bigger muscles, bigger explosions, and bigger violence.

ACTIVITY 14: **The Two Faces of Toughness**

As a teen, you've likely experienced lots of pressure to be tough and prove your toughness to other guys. You've probably noticed that sometimes the pressure to be tough is helpful, and sometimes it goes too far and isn't helpful. In the following spaces, please write down some of the pros and cons of feeling pressure to be tough in whatever way feels true for you.

Toughness Pros	Toughness Cons
Pressure to be tough is helpful when…	*Pressure to be tough goes too far when…*

I included examples from myself on the following page; circle any that you agree with.

Chris's Toughness Pros	Chris's Toughness Cons
Pressure to be tough is helpful when…	*Pressure to be tough goes too far when…*
It helps us get through life's difficult times.	Guys feel like they can never back down (which is exhausting).
It enables us to accomplish great things, work hard, and be our best.	Guys struggle to let others know when they're feeling scared or are in pain.
It leads to us feeling more confident after we've overcome challenges.	Guys feel like they can't be themselves and have to pretend (even with friends) or put on a show.
It helps us build connection with other people who we go through difficult stuff with.	Guys do things they don't really want to do.
	Guys get hurt or into trouble.

As you were circling examples, did you notice any personal memories or reflections jump into your head?

Words of Guys

Dante, a ninth-grader: In my time in wrestling practice, when I thought things were getting hard, I would, like, slow down, and my friends would be like, "Bro, just man up. Stop being a pussy." And, you know, like, "Be manly. Don't be a fag. Like, be manly—just don't be a failure." Being called a pussy is that idea of "Be manly," or if you think something is too hard… That's when "pussy" is used. When you're too scared or afraid to do something or try something, that's when I've heard it or used it.

Have you had experiences like Dante? If so, please consider if they were helpful by motivating you, hurtful by making you feel bad, or both.

Going Deeper

When it comes to what you've learned about toughness over the years, what people most represent what it means to be "tough" for you? They could be friends or family members, famous people, or even characters from a movie, book, or video game you're really into. For example, my friend Long, who fought cancer for years, truly represents toughness for me. Throughout his treatment and right up to the end, he kept doing the stuff he loved, including traveling the world and high-endurance mountaineering.

Please identify two people who represent toughness for you, and write down a few things about them that helps define "toughness" for you.

Person #1: _____

_____

_____

_____

_____

_____

_____

Person #2: _____

_____

_____

_____

_____

_____

_____

You may be aware that *lots* of adults think teen guys spend too much time playing video games… Annoying, I know. Research has identified the potential for violent video games to make some boys more aggressive and less sensitive toward others (Bartholow, Bushman, and Sestir 2006). Have you ever had any experiences that lead you to have concerns about violent video or virtual reality games?

- For example, have you ever felt more aggressive or less caring as a result of playing a game or noticed similar behavior in your friends?

- Do you have concerns about the way many male characters in these games are frequently portrayed, including megamuscles, lots of anger, and extreme violence? Why or why not?

Video games are tons of fun and help us connect with our friends, but I can remember times when I got pissed if I lost a game and controllers went flying. Some of my friends also got pretty intense and aggressive (when losing or winning). Video games can also feel pretty addictive, and it can be hard to stop playing.

By the way, I raise these questions and considerations as someone who loved Nintendo growing up (still do). I get why video games are super fun and serve as a much-needed break from reality at times.

When Risk Taking Goes Too Far

One of the primary ways that guys demonstrate "being tough" is through taking risks. I'm not talking about everyday risks that we all have to take as humans and don't think about very much, such as driving cars or riding buses. I'm talking about the higher-stakes risks—those that can lead to significant physical or emotional pain or get us into trouble—which count the most when it comes to guys proving themselves.

Higher-stakes risks can either be *calculated* or *uncalculated*. When risks are calculated, we decide in advance to do things that could be dangerous or could lead to us getting hurt (including emotionally). We take these risks because they can give us an adrenaline rush, bring about awesome feelings like excitement, and lead to "props" from other guys. Have you taken any calculated higher-stakes risks? If so, why?

Rugby was one of my calculated risks. I knew that it would often be physically painful, which it was. I knew I could get injured, which I did. But I was willing to take these risks for the excitement brought on by being part of a team battling together, overcoming physical and mental challenges, and winning. There was also a part of me that enjoyed feeling like I got more respect for playing a very physical sport.

In middle school and high school, guys start to engage in more risk taking. You may wonder why, so here are some contributing factors:

- Teens often experience increased levels of excitement in the face of risks, as opposed to adults who typically respond with caution and self-regulate (Steinberg 2014).

- Risk taking is a way to test limits, challenge adult authority, and learn about oneself; for example, *What am I up for?* versus *When does it go too far?* (Steinberg 2014).

- Select research findings indicate that the hormone testosterone, which increases for boys during puberty and adolescence, is linked to impulsivity and sensation seeking for some guys (Sapolsky 1997).

Uncalculated higher-stakes risks are those that we can't typically plan for, or that we don't plan for as well as we could. These risks include drinking alcohol at parties, doing drugs, or vandalizing things. For many teen guys, two factors that often fuel uncalculated risks include the importance of being and seeming tough (which we've been discussing) and peer pressure.

Friends and nonfriends can exert peer pressure, causing guys to feel like they have to do something to fit in or "prove" themselves. You've probably experienced this firsthand. The pressure can be *indirect*, like wanting to follow the crowd, or *direct*, like when someone gets in your face and dares you to do something. Regardless of the kind of pressure, it can be really hard to say no to things we don't want to do or aren't sure we want to do. Understandably, most teens (including me at your age) want to impress other kids, be liked, be part of the group, and avoid being made fun of.

For example, on Halloween in the eighth grade, my friend Hank brought shaving cream and eggs while we were out trick-or-treating. You can probably guess what these items were for because none of us were shaving at the time! Before I knew what was happening, he handed me an egg and dared me to toss it at a luxury car. To be honest, I didn't really want to do it, but the pressure of the group took over. So, I tossed the egg, it cracked, and then we all booked it out of there. It's complicated, right? While I didn't want to toss the egg and felt bad about doing so, it was exciting and a rush to run away and be part of the group.

Words of Guys

Howie, a tenth-grader: Like, when I hang out with them or when I used to hang out with them, when they first started doing the weed and stuff like that, if I didn't want to do it, or if I didn't want to drink, they would call me "a bitch" or "a pussy" because I didn't want to do it, and they thought I was scared to do it... If you don't want to hang out with them, or you have other stuff planned without them, then they get mad, and then they'll just bring those words up.

Have you ever experienced the type of peer pressure Howie describes? If so, what was that like, and what happened? Have you ever dished it out? (That's a "yes" for me.)

ACTIVITY 15: Getting Pressured and Being Prepared

As a teen, it can be easy to find yourself in situations you didn't prepare for. I certainly did. For instance, I remember being pressured to fight other guys and to drink at parties in high school, as well as other stuff. I'm not telling you to not take risks or to not try things out for yourself. That's for you to figure out. Experimenting is one way that many teen guys get to know themselves better and learn about their limits. However, it can be easy to end up over your head in a dangerous situation, with regrets the next day. This activity will help you do some planning so you can be more prepared when various risks arise.

The following table presents some of the risks that teen guys face, whether due to peer pressure or not. Please give each risk some thought, and then place an X for how you'd like to handle the situation. Some risks might be a definite "no way," others you may not be sure about, whereas some might sound fun and exciting and leave you "curious." If you've already taken a particular risk, feel free to mark "into it" or "not into it." It's also totally cool to answer in your head.

Risk	No Way	Not Sure	Curious	Into It or Not Into It
Trying alcohol				
Drinking lots of alcohol				
Experimenting with or doing drugs				
Smoking cigarettes				
Getting into fights				
Dares or physical challenges, like jumping off something tall				
Having unprotected sex				
Being sexually active before ready				
Sexting				
Stealing stuff				
Being part of a gang				
Skipping school				
Driving fast or dangerously				
Drinking and driving				
Vandalizing stuff, such as spray-painting or breaking windows				
Trespassing				

Great work giving this stuff some thought. For any risks for which you answered:

- "Not sure," please take a moment to think through what it is that leaves that type of risk in question for you

- "Curious," please take a moment to think through what specifically you are curious about

It's also interesting to reflect on what your "no way," "into it," or "not into it" responses mean about certain risks for you. These more definitive responses can tell you important things about yourself and what you're up for versus not.

Going Deeper

So, now for the hard part. If you decided that any of the previous risks aren't for you, whether you marked "no way," "not into it," or even "not sure," what will you do if some guys try to pressure you to do them? It's super easy for any of us to decide "I'm not into that thing" when we're just reading a book and thinking about a particular risk, but it gets much harder to stand firm in the moment, especially when the teasing and name-calling start, right? Thus, it can be helpful to think through different scenarios and prepare some responses for how you might respond in a way that's true to you.

While I wasn't the best at saying no to things as a teen guy, here are some of the responses I used at times. Please circle any that you think might be helpful for you, and feel free to add in your own next to mine.

Chris's Responses	Responses I've Used or Might Try Out
"I'm just not into that." "Not my thing." "I'm good." "No thanks." "That's more excitement than I'm up for." "I've tried it and it doesn't do it for me." "That sounds dumb." "Why don't you show us all how it's done, Bobby Big Balls?" [Can be effective, but use with caution because it adds "heat" to the situation.]	

And, of course, any time you or other guys say no to doing something risky, you gotta expect and be mentally prepared for some teasing and name-calling. It's no fun to have to deal with being called out or put down, but being prepared for it can help keep you safe and proceeding on your own terms. I remember guys in middle school and high school who were better than most at not buckling to peer pressure. I always respected those guys and their seeming confidence (compared to the rest of us) in standing firm, even when the group was piling it on them. Do you know any guys like that (it could be you)? If so, what do you think of them?

What's Your Take?

Alright, you've now had the chance to think a lot about Guy Code Rule Number Two and hopefully understand it in some new ways, especially as it relates to you. So, let's see where you stand with it.

ACTIVITY 10. Rule Number Two and You

At this point in the journey, do you think that being pressured to be tough (for example, being told to "Man up" and "Suck it up") is a problem for you or other guys you know? Why or why not?

- In particular, consider how this Guy Code Rule has worked for you and how you want to be.

- If you have mixed feelings, please reflect on the different ways that pressure to be tough, which often includes taking risks, can be helpful and harmful for you and other guys.

_____

_____

_____

_____

_____

_____

_____

_____

_____

_____

_____

Moving On

So, that sums up Rule Number Two on the importance of being tough at all times. This stuff is complicated, and everyone needs to figure out for themselves where they stand with these rules and expectations. That's what this journey is all about. As we explored, the pressure we feel to be tough has pros and cons, and we all need to be tough at times. The Guy Code can make it seem like there is only one way for us guys to be, which just isn't the case. You've now had a chance to think about how the pressure to be tough can be helpful and hurtful, and we explored some ways to say no to taking risks, if and when it comes to that. On to the next rule!

Chapter 4

Rule Number Three
Guys Should Be Players

We're now going to transition into one of the potentially more uncomfortable Guy Code Rules to explore: the pressure guys experience to be *players*, which includes "in your face" questions that many guys frequently encounter, like "Did you get some?" Chances are you're pretty familiar with this pressure. Please take a moment to notice what popped into your head as you read that first sentence…

If you're feeling any discomfort, I totally get it. Please hang in there, because this chapter covers really important topics that aren't discussed enough with teen guys, like you, as they start to navigate their own sexuality. These can be nerve-wracking times, especially if you have *no experience*—or *less* than your peers—with dating and sexual stuff. Know that you're in good company, though; this stuff is new to all of us at some point.

As you've likely encountered, and I certainly did when I was your age (even in college), guys get pressured to be players and to prove their manhood by being highly sexually active and by "hooking up" (Orenstein 2020; Smiler 2013). This pressure starts in middle school, even earlier for some boys, and increases as guys hit puberty and make their way through high school. Of course, because of the Guy Code's extreme emphasis on heterosexuality and being straight, this rule is specifically about hooking up with girls and women.

> **STOP AND THINK** *What's your understanding of being a "player" and how this pressure gets applied to guys?*

When I think of the term "player," I imagine someone who is very sexually active, is less emotionally connected to their partners, and acts more committed than they actually are. Other words used by some college guys to describe players include "attractive," "flirty," and "self-centered" (Ashmore, Del Boca, and Beebe 2002). Not to get too technical, but "player" has its roots in "playboy," an older term that your parents or caregivers are probably familiar with. A "playboy" is "a man who lives a life devoted chiefly to the pursuit of pleasure," which frequently includes lots of casual sex (Merriam-Webster, https://www.merriam-webster.com, sv "playboy").

Talking about this stuff can get confusing quickly because the language around sexuality means different things to different people. So, before we proceed any further, let's clarify some additional terms I'll be using in this chapter. "Hooking up" can mean everything from kissing and making out to sexual intercourse. For our purposes, I'll use the terms "hooking up" and "sexual experiences" to represent any of the sexual behaviors teen guys can engage in, including kissing. Alright, enough of the definitions.

I can remember lots of times growing up, especially in high school, when guys would sit around and talk about sexual experiences, asking questions like "Did you get some?" or "Did you hook up?" and oftentimes using far more explicit terminology that you can probably imagine on your own. The responses to such questions typically ranged from a "You know it" to a sheepish "No" to "None of your _____ business." The guys who responded affirmatively were celebrated and immediately asked for details, whereas guys who offered vague or negative responses were often called something like "prude" or "pussy" or, at a minimum, were met with the voicing of disappointment.

> **STOP AND THINK**
>
> *How do conversations about sex stuff go with you and your friends? Have you ever been asked questions like "Did you get some?" or "Did you hook up?"*
> *If so, do these conversations typically feel supportive or threatening, and why?*
> *If you haven't been asked such questions, please try to imagine what it might feel like. For many guys, these types of inquiries amp up the pressure to prove ourselves sexually and don't always feel great.*

So, why do guys experience pressure to be players, and where does this rule come from? Well, to begin with, many societies care a lot about heterosexuality.

This social value and preference is enforced through the pressures placed on boys and men to be straight, have lots of sex, and brag about their sexual "conquests." Some guys go along with these norms, and others not at all, with some falling in the middle. Additionally, the pressure guys experience to be players lines up with other masculinity expectations, such as calling the shots and having power over women, and acting as players (for those who do) is another way for boys and men to assert themselves.

Lastly, and let's be real here, many countries and societies around the world are run by men, and *sexism*—discrimination and prejudice related to one's sex—toward girls and women is a big problem. It makes sense that player pressure would develop and be encouraged in societies in which sexism is widespread and girls and women are treated as sexual objects.

Words of Guys

Sammie, a twelfth-grader: What a guy should be is athletic, like, smart, maybe stoic, funny, um, the guy that gets all the girls on the weekends, the guy that hooks up with the most girls on the weekends, and the guy that maybe gets drunk at parties and has a good time. Because that's viewed, I guess, as, like, what people think is attractive... I mean, if you look at a lot of rap music videos, it's like a lot of them sexually exploit women. It's all about, like, guys around gorgeous women that are half naked. Again, it's the whole image of the guy getting the girls.

Bill, a twelfth-grader: Guys are meant to be competitive with each other to find the best mate. So, we are always searching to find ways to be better than the next guy. So, if you do have sex with more girls than the other one, then, oh, you are obviously the better guy.

Do you agree with Sammie and Bill, that the guys who are most sexually active have the most status and social power? Why or why not?

This player pressure stuff is complicated. Understandably, lots of teen guys (including myself at your age) want to fit in and get props from friends and peers, which leads many of us to act like players. Player pressure can also have an appeal in and of itself; lots of people enjoy sex, and it can feel exciting and meaningful to connect with different people sexually. So, along with taking a close look at both the pros and cons of this rule to help you further establish how it's working for you, we'll explore different relationship approaches in the chapter, including how to be sexually active in respectful and safe ways (for guys who want this).

ACTIVITY 17: Player Pressure Is Everywhere

Let's hone in on some of the different ways guys receive the message that it's important to be heterosexually active and to hook up a lot. For each category in the following table, please provide one or more examples of how these things can reinforce the image of us guys as players. To help get you started, I provided examples from Jason, an eleventh-grader.

Player Pressure Categories	Examples
Media (for example, TV shows, movies, magazines, and video games)	I can think of movies that are all about guys trying to get laid, and the character Tony Stark, from Iron Man, is kind of a player. There's also Grand Theft Auto.
Other guys	A lot of guys in my high school talk about wanting to "get some" and brag about who they've been with.
Family	Whenever I see my uncle, he always asks me if I'm "dating any babes."

Do the examples you came up with bring up any reactions or feelings? Some guys might experience discomfort reflecting on the different ways that player pressure is transmitted to them, whereas other guys feel more neutral, like "It's no big deal."

Going Deeper

Interestingly, in spite of the player pressure we all receive, most guys don't actually self-identify as players or act as such in sexual or dating relationships. For example, one study found that a minority (less than 50 percent) of college guys viewed themselves as players (Smiler 2006).

So, what gives?

Based on your experiences with guys, are you surprised that more don't self-identify as players? Why or why not?

_____

_____

_____

_____

How do you identify when it comes to sexual or dating relationships? Do you consider yourself a player? Why or why not? (Feel free to respond on the lines below or in your head.)

_____

_____

_____

_____

In addition to your thoughts above, here are some possible explanations for why the majority of us guys don't end up embracing (or achieving) the player lifestyle:

- For many guys, being a player can feel unnatural and less emotionally and relationally fulfilling. So, while lots of guys talk the talk (as I did as a teen), many of us don't actually walk the walk.

- While the Guy Code is quite influential, it's not all-powerful. Guys have the ability and final authority to decide what feels right for them and how they want to be, which frequently includes wanting to be in more emotionally committed relationships (Smiler 2013).

- It's not that easy. For *most of us*, it takes mutual attraction, a fair amount of effort, and some luck for a hookup or new sexual relationship to happen. Thus, the bona fide player lifestyle isn't so easy to pull off.

Sex and Dating Can Be Scary

As you may remember from elementary school, when kids accused a classmate of having a crush or romantic interest, the response was typically a strong and very dramatic denial. What examples come to mind for you? When I was a kid, I vividly recall boys and girls, including myself, doing something called the "cootie shot" whenever one of us "accidentally" made physical contact with a person of the opposite sex (as a way to dramatically protect ourselves from the "dangerous" contact). All of this changes abruptly when *actual* crushes and dating enter the scene, usually at the start of middle school, when kids of the opposite sex start hanging out after school, going to the mall or a movie or something similar.

When crushes and dating first become a thing (usually during middle school), they can bring about lots of awkward moments and uncertainty. What comes to mind for you, whether currently or looking back, when reflecting on this period of time?

I still clearly remember how crushes, dating, and sexual stuff in middle school (and high school too) felt like really new territory...because it was! For the most part, no one talked about the newness of it or helped us guys figure out how to proceed and learn.

For instance, in sixth grade, after some friends pressured me, I abruptly asked out Samantha at the end of woodshop class. I flopped…big time. Not surprisingly, my friends ripped on me pretty badly for a while. Have you had any super awkward moments like this?

Due to the Guy Code, not many teen boys receive word that sex and dating can be pretty intimidating. This is especially true when one goes from no sexual or dating experience to having their first encounters or relationships.

I'll let you in on a secret that you've maybe already figured out for yourself: in spite of the player swagger that guys can employ, *everyone* feels nervous at times in sexual and dating situations. This is natural for anything that requires learning or is new. It can be difficult to establish this reality because many guys don't talk about their insecurity, whether they're at the hand-holding stage, kissing, or further along the spectrum. It's like we're all just supposed to know what to do and be confident, in charge, and ready to go.

You know what else? Most adults and older guys (including myself) get nervous at times when trying to get a relationship started or hooking up with someone new. Dating and sex come with lots of uncertainty and the potential for rejection, and it's straight-up vulnerable being intimate and sexual with a new person.

ACTIVITY 18: **We All Feel Nervous Sometimes**

For each of the following scenarios of teen guys navigating complicated sexual and relationship stuff, please consider the following:

- Is that guy's dilemma and uncertainty similar to anything I've encountered? If so, what?

- What advice would I give this guy if we were friends?

   Jameson, a ninth-grader: *It's the start of high school, and the extent of Jameson's prior romantic experience includes some slow dances and a very short-term relationship that involved making out. Thus, he still feels pretty inexperienced, and even more so as a ninth-grader, compared to older guys who seem really confident. Just recently he met a tenth-grade girl through working on the school newspaper and is starting to have feelings. He has no idea what to do next and is wondering if she* could ever be interested in a freshman guy like him. Jameson doesn't know how to proceed and wonders if other guys feel nervous the way he does.

Javante, a twelfth-grader: *Javante is one of the bigger kids in his grade. He has dated a little bit but hasn't had sex yet and is feeling a lot of pressure. When other guys talk about who they're "hooking up" with, he gets quiet and feels nervous that someone might put him on the spot. He did recently get questioned (in this way) and told the other kid to worry about himself and then bragged that he'd "been with plenty of girls." Aside from with his best friend Mark, who is cool and doesn't judge, Javante doesn't feel like he can be open about this stuff. He wonders if other guys also feel like they have to front, so they won't get teased and put down.*

Bo, an eighth-grader: *For several years now, Bo has become aware of feeling more attracted to guys than girls. He has started to experience pressure from other guys to prove that he's sexually interested in girls. Bo even tried to date a girl, and it didn't go anywhere. He isn't sure if he's gay, but wishes he had more ways to safely explore his sexuality and that there wasn't so much pressure to "be straight" and have it all figured out. He also wonders how his parents and other kids would respond if they knew he was questioning his sexuality.*

Dameon, an eleventh-grader: *Dameon is popular and has a lot of friends. He's known for being very sexually active and "a player." He doesn't date very much, and when he does it's shorter term. Several of his dating relationships have ended because he cheated on the other person. Dameon likes the attention and praise he gets from other guys. While it's generally fun and exciting to be sexually active with different people, it has also brought some drama and occasionally left him feeling like it might be nice to try out a longer-term relationship; but, he's not sure.*

Going Deeper

Here are some questions that frequently come up for guys in new relationships or while having a new sexual experience, including me. Please circle any you've had for yourself, or answer them in your head:

- Does this person like me like that?

- Am I gonna get rejected?

- Am I doing it the right way?

- Should I make a move, like putting my arm around them or going in for a kiss? When is the right time? Is now the right time?

- What if they don't like how I kiss or do other stuff?

- What if it's awkward?

These types of questions, and the insecurities they represent, are natural for all people, including us guys, and at all stages of sexual and dating experience. We encounter them even more often because society puts more pressure on us to be the ones to initiate romantic contact and make the first move.

Do you and your friends talk about the nervousness (and excitement) you feel over crushes or about having a new relationship or sexual experience? Hopefully you've found or will be able to find *trusted* people you can talk to about these types of questions and worries when they show up, which they will. It's no fun to be alone with this stuff; we all need people in our corner.

Don't Forget Consent

One thing I've learned is that guys are diverse in their sexual interests and approaches. While the Guy Code presents one clear model, the *player approach*, there are lots of safe and respectful ways to be sexually, from abstaining and taking your time to being more active with multiple partners (but doing so safely and being honest about intentions). It's up to you to determine what feels right for you in these types of relationships. That being said, the key ingredient for any healthy and safe romantic, sexual, or hooking-up experience is *consent*.

> *What comes up internally when you hear the word "consent"? How do you define it?*

Consent means making sure that everyone's on the same page and has verbally communicated wanting to proceed with whatever is about to happen (Orenstein 2020; Smiler 2016). While consent can be requested or provided for lots of things, it's frequently associated with sex and sexual activities. Times have changed since I was in middle school and high school, when consent was *barely discussed*. With more and more people—mostly women but also some men, trans, and nonbinary individuals—coming forward to report nonconsensual sexual encounters in which they felt victimized, consent is a very important and relevant topic for us to explore.

To get started, let's consider the barriers that can get in the way of guys, and people in general, getting consent. Some guys don't ask for consent because they're afraid they may be told no. While rejection doesn't feel good (which I can attest to), that's not a good reason to skip consent. The stakes are too high. When you inevitably are rejected, and likely will be multiple times, know that you are in good company. It's something we all experience.

For some guys, the need to ask for consent feels awkward and uncomfortable, which I get. Guys can also feel like it's "not smooth" and not how it's done on the big screen. Well, lots of things are different in reality than they are on the big screen, including how most of us guys actually are. The good news, for all of us, is that while it might feel a bit awkward, and it's not how James Bond goes about initiating sexual relations, asking for consent is super fast. An added bonus is that it leads to better communication, ensuring that everyone is on the same page in the moment. I promise you that if the other person wants "the thing" to happen, you'll get a lightning-quick yes. This affirmation just adds excitement to the situation, as it verifies that both people want the same thing.

The big downside of not asking is that there can easily be a misunderstanding or miscommunication. None of us are mind readers; if we don't ask, we don't actually know what our partners really want and are up for in the moment. Thus, by not getting consent, you may touch someone in a way they don't like, or they may feel pressured to do stuff with you they'd rather not, which is never okay.

Here are a few straightforward ways to ask for consent:

- "Can I kiss you?" [It's important to ask this, even when it's the first time.]

- "Can I touch you here?" [It helps to be specific, and it's even better to name the actual body part.]

- "Do you want to have sex?" or "Do you want to [fill in the blank]?" [Consent applies to everything, not just sex.]

- "What would feel good for you tonight? What are you up for?" [This is a great way to get a conversation started, and then you can also answer the questions yourself. When you're with someone longer term, you can *decide together* how you want to go about consent.]

> **STOP AND THINK**
>
> *There are lots of ways to ask for consent. How might you ask for consent in a way that feels natural and authentic (whether using the previous examples or a phrase of your own making)?*

Of course, when someone initiates intimacy or sexual contact with you, they should also get your consent. Guys need to feel onboard and okay with whatever is happening too.

ACTIVITY 19: Player Problems

There is nothing wrong with wanting to be sexually active and to have multiple experiences safely and respectfully. Yet the significant pressure most guys encounter to be players can lead to problems that are important to be aware of and anticipate. For the following list of problems, please circle "yes," "no," or "kind of" if you've experienced the issue or know a guy who has. It's also fine to answer in your head.

Player pressures become a problem when:

- Guys feel badly about themselves because they aren't able to live up to expectations to have lots of sexual partners, or it feels unnatural to want lots of sex.

  Yes | No | Kind of

  Possible solution: As we'll explore further, there are lots of ways to be in romantic and sexual relationships, so do your best to embrace what feels right for you.

- Guys feel like they need to rush into things, like dating or sexual experiences, as opposed to going at their own pace.

  Yes | No | Kind of

  Possible solution: Similar to the previous solution.

- Guys feel like they can't be real and talk to others about nervousness because of social pressures that emphasize being in control and a "stud."

  Yes | No | Kind of

  Possible solution: Hopefully, you have or can find some friends whom you can trust and be open with. We all need that!

- Guys can be so focused on hooking up or having sex that they don't get consent, or they feel like they deserve it, which can lead to all sorts of *very bad* outcomes.

  Yes | No | Kind of

  Possible solution: Practice getting consent and make the commitment to yourself to always get consent.

- Guys talk about or treat girls and women like sexual objects (for example, "I'd like to tap that ass" and "Did you get some?"). This is also known as *objectification*.

  Yes | No | Kind of

  Possible solution: I did plenty of this as a teen guy, which I regret. It leads to girls and women being disrespected and treated as sexual objects whose primary purpose is to provide pleasure. If this issue resonates with you, a first step to consider is to stop treating girls as sexual objects yourself (which takes practice). The harder step is to take a stand and let other guys know when they're being offensive and demeaning. This isn't easy to do; see chapter 7 for some tips on taking a stand.

Going Deeper

Something else that contributes to player pressure is pornography. While plenty of guys don't use porn, most teenage boys will see it eventually, and some quite a lot (Wright, Paul, and Herbenick 2021).

I'm guessing that you're hearing words of caution about porn from adults, whether at school or at home, so I'll keep this discussion brief. The information in this section is really just meant as an FYI, so do with it what you will.

The main thing I want to emphasize, and something more and more teen guys (and maybe you too) are becoming aware of, is that most heterosexual pornography represents sexual behaviors and relationships in unrealistic ways. This porn:

- Frequently presents men as aggressive, dominant, and emotionally disconnected

- Portrays women as primarily passive recipients or "pleasure providers," as opposed to equal partners

Most importantly for you to know, these unrealistic representations give many teen boys *the wrong idea* about how they should be and what it's actually like to be in sexual and romantic relationships that involve mutual communication and a desire to figure out what each person wants and is into. Porn can also be addictive and contributes to a higher risk of sexual aggression and assault (Wright, Paul, and Herbenick 2021).

If you're not already aware, a newer type of pornography called "ethical porn" is becoming more popular. Its makers strive to focus on realistic and respectful representations of sex (Scott 2016). For anyone wanting to view pornography with more accurate representations of sex, this is a better option to go with.

That's all I want to say on porn, and thanks for bearing with me. I can't remember any adults talking to me about porn or the ways it frequently misrepresents sex between people. Unfortunately, this lack of discussion is pretty common. So, as much as it may feel awkward, annoying, and uncomfortable, if an adult makes the effort to talk about this stuff, hear them out, and then decide for yourself what makes sense for you and how you want to proceed.

Lots of Guys Want Commitment

Just as many guys can feel insecure and nervous about stuff involving sex and relationships, something else not widely acknowledged is that lots of teen boys want to be in committed relationships (Smiler 2013). This certainly wasn't the thing my friends and I discussed in middle school and high school. We talked about crushes, physical attraction, and wanting to "get some action" because we were socialized that way.

What are you most interested in commitment-wise? Do you have a preference for dating more casually, wanting a more committed and longer-term relationship, or neither, and why?

While there are plenty of guys, and people of all genders, interested in having a greater number of sexual experiences with less focus on commitment, there are also lots of teen guys who value emotionally connected relationships that are longer-term and exclusive, meaning you only see or have sexual experiences with each other. However, many guys don't know this. It doesn't get talked about much because of player pressure, which contributes to lots of guys understandably worrying that if they bring up their desire for commitment, they'll get ripped on (Orenstein 2020).

Max, a first-year college student: I was raised to be, like, accepting and just open–minded about different types of people. It, like, doesn't matter if a guy is, like, gay or hasn't had sex by the time he's eighteen or whatever. It doesn't matter. Like, everybody is still a human being when it comes down to it, and we all have that in common.

In comparison to Max, what have you been taught about guys and sex? How has that influenced what you're all about today with regard to guys and player pressure?

ACTIVITY 20: Sex and Dating... What Are You All About?

There are lots of ways to be when it comes to dating and sexual relationships. Here are a few common approaches. As you read through them, please consider whether any feel like a fit for you. If not, there's a blank space at the bottom for you to describe your own unique approach.

Approach	Description
Just wanna have fun	This guy is not looking to be in a committed relationship. He wants to have different sexual experiences, and not necessarily with one partner at a time. He also values the learning that happens from diverse sexual experiences. While having no qualms about being uncommitted, he cares about the people he's with, feels emotionally connected to them, and is direct and open about wanting to be in a more "open" relationship.
All in and looking for commitment	This guy wants to be in a committed relationship. He's looking for commitment and someone he feels emotionally connected to and has fun with. He's excited to be intimate and gain more experience sexually with a partner he gets to know better. [Remember, gaining more experience sexually can mean lots of things.]

Approach	Description
Player	This guy is very similar to "just wanna have fun" guy. However, two key differences exist. As a "player," he's less direct and honest with partners about wanting an uncommitted and open relationship. He also tries to not get emotionally connected to partners nor care about them beyond their sexual purposes.
Not interested	This guy isn't currently interested in having sexual experiences or intimate relationships. It's not his thing, which is totally cool. He doesn't feel ready, and he'd rather be doing other stuff. This might change at some point, or it might not.
None of these describe me...but this does	

My main approach in high school—and beyond—was "all in and looking for commitment." For me, that has always felt the most comfortable. I also tried out "just wanna have fun," and it didn't fit me very well. There are lots of ways to be, and many guys need to experiment before figuring out what they're all about.

Going Deeper

For the sex and dating approach (or approaches) that resonates with you, please consider what specifically works for you or feels right about it, and then write your thoughts down. Feel free to also reflect more generally on the type of guy and partner you aspire to be in sexual or romantic relationships.

_____

_____

_____

_____

_____

For the approach (or approaches) that didn't resonate with you, please consider what specifically felt off or not right about it, and then write your thoughts down.

_____

_____

_____

_____

_____

What's Your Take?

Alright, you've now had the chance to go deeper into Guy Code Rule Number Three. Because of how media portrays sex and sexuality, including guys as players, and because of the expectations that society places on us, this rule can be very complicated to navigate. As always, this exploration is about you finding your own way and what works for how you want to be. So, let's see where you stand.

ACTIVITY 21: Rule Number Three and You

At this point in the journey, do you think that guys being pressured to be players is a problem for you or other guys? Why or why not?

- In particular, consider how this rule has worked for you and how you want to be.

- If you have mixed feelings, please identify the pros and cons of being a player, both for you and other guys.

_____

_____

_____

_____

_____

_____

_____

_____

_____

_____

_____

Moving On

For many of us, exploring sexuality and player pressure can get uncomfortable and be confusing. Way to go sticking with it! One of the reasons these topics can be so difficult to explore is that they aren't frequently discussed in ways that allow us to be vulnerable. Yet they are incredibly important, highly relevant issues that impact all of us guys. I appreciate you taking a closer look at the ways guys get pressured to be players, as well as some of the potential consequences of buying into this rule, including guys feeling like they have to front or treat girls like sexual objects. You've now cracked the code on this one and are hopefully better positioned to decide how you want to be and what feels best for you. Let's keep moving!

Chapter 5

Rule Number Four

Guys Should Call the Shots and Be Alphas

When I've talked to teen boys about masculinity pressures, a term they frequently mention is "alpha male." Lots of guys see examples of alpha males in famous actors and sports stars, and they can also come into contact with guys who take on the role of alphas in their communities, like some fathers and coaches.

 What does "alpha male" mean to you? Do any specific characteristics or people come to mind when you think of the term?

For me, the term "alpha male" immediately brings forth the image of a chimpanzee, specifically the biggest and most domineering of the group, like Caesar, the leader of the chimps in *Planet of the Apes*. For most of us guys, an alpha male is someone who has the most status and power. Alpha males are the guys who call the shots and decide who gets to be "in" and who is "out." Alpha males are also frequently big, strong, and really good at stuff the group cares about, like sports and being tough. While meanness can be a part of the alpha male role, it doesn't have to be. Guys take on this role in all different ways.

When I was in middle school, Brant was the clear alpha male for our class. He was bigger than all of us and really good at sports, especially the more physical ones like ice hockey and football. He went through puberty early, started dating and hooking up sooner, and hung out with older kids. Brant could also be a bully (not a requirement for being an alpha male, by the way), and he had a crew that followed him around. I hung out with Brant and his crew sometimes and was always on edge because you never knew when a "dead arm" (that is, being punched really hard in the arm) or diss could come your way.

Research Moment

Boys start to pick up on the societal preference for them to be domineering and in charge at a young age. Some guys even begin to assert themselves in alpha ways in kindergarten or earlier. For example, in one kindergarten class, a boy named Mikey started the "Mean Team" and decided which guys could join while enforcing a "No girls allowed" rule (Chu 2014). Did you have any similar experiences in elementary school or even more recently? If so, what were they like?

So, why do guys experience pressure to be alpha males who call the shots, and where does this rule come from? Well, in lots of ways being an alpha male represents different Guy Code Rules coming together as part of society's vision of the "ideal boy or man": a guy who is tough, is domineering, is emotionally in control, and gives orders and is listened to. You may be thinking, *Well, that sounds like a pretty good way to be*, and it can be for those guys who pull it off without being mean to others and getting all bossy.

Additionally, though societal change is happening, men still run most things, from countries to companies. Thus, alpha male pressure also serves to uphold the "patriarchy," the societal structure that keeps boys and men in higher-status positions with more power and privilege (and white boys and men even more so in European countries and the United States).

Along with outside pressure, some guys aspire to be alphas because it just feels good:

- It can feel empowering and self-esteem boosting to be the leader, to be the one calling the shots, and to have the type of influence that leads others to listen to you and look to you for guidance.

- When one is in charge (whether it's a club at school, a company, or a sports team), there is the potential to have an impact on and contribute to something bigger than yourself, like winning a game, making money, or helping address a social or global problem.

- From a purely Guy Code standpoint, being the alpha validates that you're meeting the societal standard for how guys are expected to be.

Not to be a downer, but it's important to acknowledge that the pressure guys experience to be alphas can set them up for disappointment. Why, you might ask? Well, a limited number of guys get to be alpha males and truly call the shots, which means *a lot* of us won't be able to achieve such "status." Furthermore, no guy can always be in charge. So, if you are the top guy in one setting, there will inevitably be other settings in which other guys, or people, will run the show.

Words of Guys

Matt, a twelfth-grader: It's the alpha male type of thing. That's exactly what it is. So, they want other people to be submissive to them. They want to exert their power. You know what I'm saying? So, they kind of want to bring you down a few notches to raise them up a few—like to make them look a little better, and that's definitely why they do it... I feel like a lot of guys want to get the edge over another guy. They're, um, pretty competitive in nature, especially here at this school.

Luis, a tenth-grader: I think just because guys like to be in each other's face a lot. They like to either bring one another down or boss... I think it comes from an instinct of wanting to be the alpha male, from wanting to be the top dog... I've realized, you know, guys are kind of just like this always. Always wanting to be tough, always wanting to be the best, always wanting to be number one.

Do you agree with Matt and Luis's assessments of why guys try to be alpha and dominate one another? Why or why not? Have you experienced alpha male pressure yourself?

ACTIVITY 22: Alpha Male Ingredients

A lot of things can go into guys trying to be an alpha male, or "the man." Here's a list of the more common alpha male ingredients that also connect to the other Guy Code Rules. Please circle any that you relate to and that feel important, and cross out any that don't matter to what you're all about. If you feel like I left out any ingredients, please add them in the open spaces.

Alpha Male Ingredients
Call the shots
Don't ask for help
Be strong and lift weights
Be great at sports
Hook up (with girls/women)
Don't show vulnerable emotions
Act tough and take risks
Appear very confident
Be supercompetitive and win a lot
Be physically dominant
Put other guys down verbally

Please take a moment to consider why the ingredients you circled are more important to you than those you crossed out. As a teen, I remember caring lots about *all* of these aspects of being an alpha male, while also experiencing the inevitable disappointment when I was unable to live up to them.

Going Deeper

In spite of the pressure to be an alpha, plenty of guys aren't that interested in trying to take on the role. It doesn't feel natural, and they are fine with other guys being more dominant and in charge, especially when they're nice about it. If you identify as a guy who cares about and wants to be an alpha male, please answer the questions that go with #1. If you're a guy who really isn't that interested, please answer the question that goes with #2.

1. Do you have any spaces or situations in which you call the shots and take on the role of alpha male? If so, how does it feel to take on that role? What type of alpha are you, and why is being one important to you?

2. What has contributed to you caring less or not at all about being an alpha male?

_____

_____

_____

_____

_____

_____

_____

_____

The Different Shades of Alpha

Alpha guys take on the role in many different ways. While calling the shots and being the dominant person in the group are requirements (Levant et al. 2012), there are plenty of guys who execute the role in kinder ways. For example:

- There are guys in leadership positions, such as heads of companies or coaches, team captains, or presidents of clubs at school, who have the final say over decisions and who go out of their way to listen to others, welcome different perspectives, and communicate clearly about the decisions they make instead of employing the more dismissive "Because I said so."

- There are leaders who acknowledge when they don't know the answer, which supports a more cooperative vibe and team culture.

- There are devoted dads in more traditional households who take pride in supporting the needs of their family beyond just the financial. While it's clearly established that these more traditional dads have "the final say," they welcome questions and talk through issues and family matters with their loved ones.

When I was twelve years old and at sleepaway camp, I encountered an older camper, Dylan, who was a true leader. I also thought Dylan was so cool. He was one of the strongest guys at camp, very popular, and really good at sports. Not surprisingly, he appeared incredibly confident and "smooth." I don't remember him ever being mean. While Dylan had no problem speaking up and was a natural leader, he did so respectfully and took time to listen to other guys. He was also funny and joked around. For me, Dylan represented the way alpha males should be, and I learned a lot from him.

 Have any older-teen male mentors influenced you? If so, in what ways? Can you think of other examples of effective alpha male leadership?

Effective alpha leadership of all different shades has the potential to contribute to incredible innovations and outcomes. The world needs people to step up, lead, and make things happen, right? That's how change occurs and how transformational inventions like the internet and smartphones and better gaming systems are developed. Furthermore, during crises (including wars and natural disasters) and in response to other social emergencies (like racism and poverty), leaders need to be forceful, bold, and quick to make decisions and take action, all of which are alpha qualities.

Words of Guys

Demetrius, a ninth-grader, provides his own take on alpha male qualities:

[*Being the alpha male*] means walking around with, like, a lot of swag. It's like, walk around with, like, your head high and being positive... It's having, like, the coolness to you that people just can see without even talking to you... It's like people come up to you and say, "Hi," and give you a high five or something like that.

What do you notice when you compare Demetrius's words to the descriptions from Matt and Luis earlier in the chapter? In your opinion, can guys who take a more "positive" approach to other people still be alphas?

ACTIVITY 23: Being a More Agreeable Alpha

In the previous activity, we reviewed the more standard ingredients associated with alpha males, everything from dominating others and calling the shots to being strong and not asking for help. And, we just explored some of the ways that it's possible to go about being the alpha more nicely and collaboratively. So, how do those more agreeable alphas pull it off and balance authority and calling the shots with collaboration and teamwork?

Here are a few of the characteristics of agreeable alphas:

- They're good listeners.

- They value the perspectives and input of others.

- They acknowledge when they don't have the answer.

Let's take a moment to explore other traits that more agreeable alphas exhibit. First, please identify three alphas of any gender whom you've experienced as commanding alpha-level respect, but doing so in a nicer and more cooperative way. These could be folks you know or famous people. For example, NBA player LeBron James seems to walk this line effectively. He is tough and dominant on the court, gives lots of money to charity, cares about his teammates, and is a devoted dad.

Agreeable alpha #1: _____

Agreeable alpha #2: _____

Agreeable alpha #3: _____

Next, brainstorm: What is it about these people that makes them agreeable alphas and effective leaders? Try to come up with at least three specific traits (in addition to what's previously listed) that distinguish them from more traditional, less-agreeable alphas.

Agreeable Alpha Traits
1.
2.
3.
4.

Though being an alpha isn't for everyone, if you're a guy who wants to be one, but do so more nicely and cooperatively, the list you just created should help you get started.

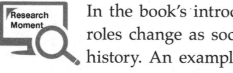

Research Moment In the book's introduction, we explored how gender and gender roles change as societies evolve, and through the progression of history. An example of such change is that the assumption that only men take on alpha roles, such as running companies or playing professional sports, is no longer acceptable (at least in many spaces and communities). Women have been in the workforce for a long time, proving that they are just as capable as men in alpha roles. They now call the shots for some of the biggest companies in the world, including CVS, General Motors, Citigroup, and UPS (Connett 2021; Kimmel 2016).

Going Deeper

It's not possible for us all to be alpha males (even the nicer variety), but there are lots of ways to be a guy who steps up and makes a difference for others—even if you're not an alpha. If being this type of guy resonates with you, please take a moment to think about and respond to these questions.

Reflect on a time when you rose to the occasion and helped out another person who needed it. What enabled you to take action like that?

_____

_____

_____

_____

To support stepping up and taking action, is there something you'd like to commit to doing in the coming week or month to help out another person who could use it? You could also commit to a specific cause. Please write down any ideas here. (If nothing comes to mind, you can always be on the lookout for these types of opportunities.)

_____

_____

_____

_____

Guys Who Take It Too Far

Perhaps you're familiar with the phrase "Don't be that guy" and have even used it yourself. Well, guys who take calling the shots and trying to be alpha too far can get themselves into "Don't be that guy" territory.

Have you ever used the phrase "Don't be that guy," or had it used against you, whether playfully or more harshly? If so, what examples come to mind? How did it feel to use the phrase or have it used in relation to you?

The phrase "Don't be that guy" has lots of uses. It can be used to call out guys who are doing foolish or embarrassing things, or are trying too hard. For example, I'm sure you've seen a guy really working it to "be smooth" with girls or trying to make sure others think he's an alpha (such as by slamming weights to the floor at the gym and then grunting). I also remember guys in high school and college, including myself at times, who tried to be alpha by outdrinking others at parties and instead ended up getting "sloppy."

Sometimes, when guys such as dads or older brothers aren't able to be alpha males on bigger stages, such as at work or at school, they compensate by calling the shots and acting alpha in their homes (and typically in the less agreeable way). For example, when I was a teenager I bossed my younger brother around and physically dominated him (until he got bigger than me). I was *that guy*. Why do guys do things like this? Well, we receive a lot of social pressure to be dominant, in control, and listened to. For plenty of us, it feels like we're doing something wrong, or we aren't worthy, if we struggle to dominate others or our peers don't really listen to us. So, finding a way to be an alpha on a smaller stage, as I did with my brother, can partly restore pride and self-esteem. The technical term for this is *overcompensation*, which you may be familiar with.

Words of Guys

Here are some alpha descriptors from **Drew, a first-year college student:**

Masculine behavior includes not caring about what other people think, um, doing stuff for yourself, being selfish, um, being aggressive and big, um, I don't know, being an asshole.

Do you agree with Drew, that being "masculine" and an alpha means "not caring about what other people think" and "being an asshole"? If so, how do you feel about "asshole" behavior being considered masculine and something society expects us guys to engage in?

ACTIVITY 24: **Don't Be *That Guy***

When guys stray into "Don't be that guy" territory, it can create problems for them and other people. Read each of the following examples and consider what comes to mind. Perhaps you've been "that guy" yourself, or know someone who has. For all of us, life is about learning and making adjustments. Most of us will have done some of these things and may still be struggling with being "that guy." So, please come up with a possible solution for each behavior in question, whether for yourself or for someone you know.

When "calling the shots" is taken too far, it can lead one to…

1. Act bossy and not listen to others

Possible solution: _____

_____

_____

2. Believe that girls/women and people of other genders shouldn't also call the shots

Possible solution: _____

_____

_____

3. Not seek input from trusted people when challenges arise

Possible solution: _____

_____

_____

4. Pretend they know what they're doing when they really don't

Possible solution: _____

_____

_____

Some guys engage in the previous behaviors a lot, and many of us engage in them at times, sometimes unintentionally. I engaged in number 4 the most as a teenager, like the time I rode my friend's dirt bike into some bushes because I didn't first ask him to show me how to use it. Whoops!

Going Deeper

Some boys and men frequently dominate conversations (Solnit 2008), which is another example of striving to be the alpha. What does this look like? Well, it happens when a guy answers a question or explains something in a very one-sided way that leaves little room for others to contribute, and their way of talking often includes cutting the other person off when they try to speak. Girls and women experience this frequently, because some guys assume that they don't know anything about what's being discussed or have little to contribute. I've unintentionally engaged in this form of communication at times, and it's something I've worked on not doing.

Do you know any guys who dominate conversations, or do you yourself? Can you think of any conversations you've had when it wasn't easy to get a word in and the other person didn't seem all that interested in what you had to say? What was that like? Most of us don't enjoy being on the other end of these types of one-sided exchanges.

Because of alpha male pressure, this can be an easy trap for us guys to fall into. If you don't want to be a guy who dominates others in conversation, consider:

- Setting the goal for yourself to have more balanced back-and-forth conversations. Some helpful responses to try out: "What do you think about [this issue]?" "It would be cool to hear your thoughts." "While I feel differently, good to know where you're coming from."

- Practicing listening. It's easy to formulate our responses to someone while they're talking rather than really trying to understand what they're saying (especially when we disagree). Work on taking it all in and pausing before responding.

- Checking in with yourself quickly during a conversation: *Am I doing a good job of listening to this person and showing interest?*

- Noticing when you interrupt. We all do this accidentally sometimes, and people appreciate a quick "Sorry, I didn't mean to interrupt" when it happens.

All of these things take practice and you wanting to change. With time, you'll develop a greater mindfulness and awareness of how you behave in conversations, and how you come across to others. It's a process. For guys wanting to go even deeper, do a quick internet search on "mindful listening strategies."

Asking for Help

Are you familiar with the classic stereotype of the guy who's lost but refuses to ask for directions, so he continues to be lost and still won't ask for directions? While this example is a bit dated, since we now just plug destinations into our smartphones, it represents a key consequence—not asking for help—of the pressure us guys receive to be alpha males who call the shots.

Why is calling the shots at odds with asking for help? Perhaps it's obvious. When us guys ask for help, we immediately give power to the other person by acknowledging that they have expertise or knowledge—such as about a confusing topic at school or a relationship issue—that we don't. It also communicates that we're unable to handle a situation or issue on our own. While asking for help isn't a big deal for some guys, plenty of teen boys (and men) struggle with it due to alpha pressures to be in charge and in control at all times (DeBate, Gatto, and Rafal 2018).

STOP AND THINK *Do you struggle with asking for help? If so, can you think of any times you didn't ask for help when you really could have used it (including more recently)?*

I remember plenty of times that I didn't ask for help when I should have, such as when I was thirteen and cut my foot badly doing something foolish with a glass. I tried to bandage it up on my own using duct tape (yes, really), only to be whisked off to the emergency room when my parents figured out what had happened.

Guys commonly struggle with asking for help from:

- Doctors (for issues that don't require immediate attention)

- Therapists (when feeling badly on the inside)

- Teachers (when they're having difficulties with a subject)

- Friends or caregivers (when needing emotional or other support)

When guys don't ask for help, problems can arise. Here are some common ones:

- Grades go down at school because you aren't receiving adequate support.

- Mental health challenges, like depression or anxiety, worsen (DeBate, Gatto, and Rafal 2018).

- Health issues go untreated, which often leads to complications (Courtenay 2011).

- Feelings of loneliness and crappiness develop (or persist) because you're trying to deal with problems alone that no one else knows about (Kindlon and Thompson 1999).

Have you or guys you know experienced any of these challenges?

ACTIVITY 25: When Guys Don't Ask for Help

I think that most people agree that, in spite of the difficulties many guys have asking for help, we all need support and assistance at times. We can only know so much, and there are certain issues, like medical issues, school problems, and all sorts of personal and relationship challenges, that just get worse if we don't have people in our corner. Let's explore some ways that guys can ask for help.

For each of the following difficult situations, circle the options you think might best serve the guy in question. Feel free to write down your own ideas in the blank spaces.

Derrick, a tenth-grader, *recently experienced the death of his uncle Anthony. They were really close. Derrick is an only child, and his uncle Anthony took him on camping trips every summer. He also lived close by, so they saw one another a lot. His death was unexpected and caught everyone by surprise. It has now been four months since his uncle's death, and Derrick continues to struggle with sleep, attention in school, and getting assignments done. He also hasn't* *felt like hanging out with friends. Derrick's parents try to check in, and it's difficult for him to put into words what's going on and how he's feeling.*

- Tell his parents what's going on

- Talk to his friends about how he's feeling

- Meet with a therapist

- Other: _____

  _____

Julio, a twelfth-grader, *is in his last year of high school. He barely passed eleventh grade, and his grades have gone down every year of high school. Julio has an older brother, and as a result, he's been invited to parties with older teens since he was a ninth-grader. Julio's parents both work two jobs, and, for a while now, it's been hard for them to be around and do stuff with him. What started out as occasional drinking and smoking pot has turned into smoking every day and partying most weekends. While Julio enjoys having fun, he feels like his substance use is getting out of control. For instance, he has noticed that he feels anxious and can't fall asleep without smoking. He worries that his grades have gotten so bad that he won't get into college.*

- Tell his parents about his concerns

- Talk to his friends or brother about what's going on

- Meet with a school counselor for support

- Other: _____

  _____

Mel, a seventh-grader, *is struggling in school. For a long time he has noticed that the letters get mixed up in his head when he reads. This also happens with numbers in math. More recently, Mel has noticed that school is getting harder with more reading assignments, and he's getting Cs and Ds. His older sister, Cassie, is one of the best students in high school. Mel's parents constantly comment on how proud they are of her, while telling him that he "just needs* *to work harder," which makes him feel crappy. Mel is feeling like he really needs some help, but he's embarrassed and self-conscious.*

- Tell his parents how he gets words and numbers mixed up

- Talk to his friends about his struggles

- Request extra help from his teachers

- Other: _____

_____

Going Deeper

Not asking for help or admitting when we're struggling to handle things on our own places us guys in a bind. It's inevitable that we'll all need help from others at times. Life's complicated, and we can only know and do so much for ourselves. So, when us guys don't ask for help, it's actually harder for us to succeed and do well, which leads to us being unhappy.

If you have difficulty asking for help, here are some tips that can make doing so a little easier. Please circle any that you've used or would considering using, and write in any additional ideas in the blank spaces:

- Give yourself permission to be a guy who asks for help and isn't "too big" to need the support of others at times.

- Remind yourself that not getting help when you need it makes life harder and less enjoyable. (This is true for all of us.)

- Find people you trust to be in your *inner circle.* Whether you choose caregivers, extended family members, friends, siblings, or male mentors, this circle should only include people whom you trust and can turn to when life inevitably gets tough. "Trust" is the big word here, because, as we know, confiding in the wrong person can lead to teasing and meanness.

- Remember the times you provided help to others, and remind yourself that all people need and are deserving of help, including you!

- With few exceptions, professional helpers (like doctors, counselors, and even teachers) can keep things that you share private, which you can confirm with them at your first meeting.

- _____

- _____

- _____

What's Your Take?

Nice work sticking with Guy Code Rule Number Four. You got to think more deeply about the pressure guys experience to be alpha males, as well as some of the outcomes of trying to be the alpha—good and bad. So, let's see where you stand.

ACTIVITY 26: Rule Number Four and You

At this point in the journey, do you think that pressure to be an alpha who calls the shots is an issue for you or other guys? Why or why not?

- In particular, consider how this rule has worked for you and how you want to be.

- If you have mixed feelings, please identify the pros and cons of this rule for you and other guys.

_____

_____

_____

_____

_____

_____

_____

_____

_____

_____

_____

_____

_____

Moving On

Four down and two more to go! You're now more than halfway done with our exploration of the Guy Code Rules. That's awesome! You're getting to think about issues that impact all guys but that most of us aren't invited to consider much, like how the pressure to be an alpha male who calls the shots has influenced you, and how striving to be an alpha can sometimes go too far. Many of us also aren't told that following the Guy Code, or parts of it, is a choice, which means you get to decide what works for you and what doesn't.

Chapter 6

Rule Number Five

Guys Should Play Sports—School... Not So Much

All of us guys get the message pretty early on, as young as three years old, that certain activities are for guys and others aren't: "That's for _____." Of course, the word that most frequently fills that blank space is "girls." While the Guy Code (and society) endorses certain activities, like sports, as being more "manly," others, such as dress-up and art, are categorized as being "for girls."

> **STOP AND THINK** *In your experience, what activities are guys encouraged to do and discouraged from doing?*

Guys commonly receive the message to stay away from "girl activities," which include things like theater, dance, singing, reading, and school-related stuff. As far as "guy activities" go, sports get the most press and are what we are most encouraged and pressured to do. Society also encourages boys to roughhouse, build things, play outdoors, play video games, and engage in games that revolve around battles, running, and physical activity (along with other stuff).

I don't know about you, but I enjoyed a lot of these activities growing up. I have great memories of playing outside with my siblings, doing everything from running around and building forts to playing all sorts of different ball games. I clearly remember the smells of dirt, grass, and trees while at play outside, and of rain on the concrete while playing basketball.

So, why do guys experience so much pressure to play sports and excel at them and to downgrade other activities? Well, as might be obvious, the activities that society encourages us to do align with the Guy Code and allow us to prove our "manhood" and that we belong. For instance, with sports, especially the more physical ones like football, hockey, basketball, and lacrosse, guys are able to:

- Prove physical toughness and that they can handle challenges

- Demonstrate muscular strength

- Elevate their status by outperforming other guys

- Exhibit mental toughness

- Be competitive and hopefully win

On the other hand, the "girl activities," including stuff related to school, don't align with masculinity pressures and the ways the Guy Code wants us to be. (More to come on that later, especially the pressure we receive to take school less seriously.)

Excelling at sports is one of the ways guys quickly gain status and social acceptance, especially if they're really good at more physical sports (Messner 1995). Not all sports are treated equal, that's for sure. In high school, I remember that the new guys who transferred in and were good at sports like football, hockey, and basketball received instant credibility and made friends more easily than other new kids. Besides being accepted more quickly, by engaging in the "right" activities and proving themselves at sports, teen guys can also distance themselves from the ultimate insults: being called "a girl" or "gay."

Let me be clear: I'm not implying that participating in sports is bad. The previous list contains traits, such as competitiveness and mental and physical toughness, that can be helpful in life for all people. Not to mention that sports are fun and offer benefits like fitness, learning teamwork, and learning about commitment (for example, to practice and get better). It's the extreme pressure that guys feel to play sports that can be problematic, especially if they end up feeling like they *can't do* other stuff of interest or they *pretend* to be into sports to please and gain acceptance from others.

The "school is uncool" thing, a consequence of the Guy Code's extreme emphasis on sports, can also be problematic for guys who take this rule to heart. I went through a period of such thinking in middle school and ended up with all Cs and Ds and very unhappy parents. Specifically, the societal messages many of us guys receive about school, such as *It's not cool to try hard* and *School is more for girls*, put us in a really tough position. There can be big, lifelong consequences for guys who don't do well in school. The stakes are high, as we'll explore.

Cody, a twelfth-grader: Well, you're an outcast because the clothes you wear, the things you like, um, because you're not good at sports. Those are some of the main things I would say… Um, as far as in the eyes of guys, at least, the most unacceptable one would be, kind of, like, the sensitive guys. Those are the ones who are called "feminine," "fag," stuff like that. They don't like sports, or they're kind of, just like, inside basement dwellers if you will… Anything unacceptable would, kind of, be floating toward the more feminine girl side of things.

Thomas, an eighth-grader: Um, in my opinion, it's the whole idea of being the alpha male, of being the guy who does sports, who's athletic, because you get to show your power and your strength. And um, maybe that's not your suit, and your suit is theater or singing. But, really, it's the male concept of being strong, and I think that's really all in a guy's head. And that's instinct.

Do you agree with Cody and Thomas about the importance of playing sports for guys over other activities? Please also reflect on any experiences you've had with being pressured to do certain activities and not others, and what that was like.

ACTIVITY 27: School, Sports, and Me

Pretty much all guys will experience pressure to play and do well at sports. Additionally, most of us guys will receive the message that school is less valued, that it's more of a "girl thing," and that we should act like we don't care about it.

So, let's take a look at how school and sports stack up for you. Please complete the following prompts in whatever way is true for you, with the goal of answering why you like or don't like sports and school.

For me, school is: _____

_____

_____

_____

_____

For me, sports are: _____

_____

_____

_____

_____

What's your level of interest with sports versus school, and what's your understanding of where your preferences come from? Who, if anyone, has influenced how you feel about sports and school?

Going Deeper

The pressure guys feel to "crush it" when it comes to sports, and to look down on school and other "girl activities," can lead many of us to steer clear of certain activities and experiences. This is only a problem if you end up missing out on something that could have been really fun or meaningful. In lots of cases, you'll never know.

However, sometimes we *do know*, and we started an activity that was fun and felt important only to stop because of pressure from others, such as parents, caregivers, or other guys. Please take a moment to reflect on whether you have ever experienced anything like this, and if so, list what you gave up:

_____   _____

_____   _____

_____   _____

If it feels important to you to give any of the activities you gave up another try, please circle them. Then, write in below any activities you've been curious about trying but haven't had the chance to yet.

_____   _____

_____   _____

_____   _____

Guys Are Into All Sorts of Stuff

As clear as the Guy Code is about what types of stuff we're allowed to do and which activities will help us prove that we are tough, strong, and able to handle pressure, guys are _diverse_. What do I mean by that? Well, guys are into lots of different stuff, some of which is "Guy Code-approved," and plenty of which isn't. Just look around. From farmers and nurses to dancers and artists to rugged athletes, guys have a lot going on, and there are a lot of things we're good at.

So, despite all the pressure we experience to be a certain way, we don't all end up doing or liking the same stuff. That's really important to acknowledge, because while masculinity pressures are quite powerful, _they aren't all-powerful_. Lots of guys are into activities other than sports, including things considered "for girls."

As a teen, I actually did a lot of stuff on the "not for guys" list, along with plenty of things that are. For instance, English literature and history were my favorite subjects (because they came more easily to me). I sang in the choir and was part of a community service club. I played lots of sports, but not the higher-status ones. Some of these activities led to teasing at times, which many of us guys experience and have to deal with.

Have you ever been teased for doing something that's considered more for girls? If so, what was that like? Have you ever teased someone else for the same reason, and if so, what comes to mind?

ACTIVITY 28: Guy Code Activities and What You're Into

The following list of activities are those that society typically categorize as more appropriate for boys or girls. Circle any that you enjoy doing or are curious about trying. Feel free to write in any additional activities that I left out that are important to you. Then, for each activity, place a check mark in the column you think it goes with the most based on societal expectations.

Activity	More for Guys	More for Girls
Playing sports		
Fashion or clothes shopping		
Cooking or baking		
Art (including pottery, photography, and sculpture)		
Video games		
Choir and singing		
School and academics in general		
Mathematics		
Creative writing		
Science		
Language arts/English		
Roughhousing and wrestling		
Theater (including acting and dance)		
History		
Playing outside		

Activity	More for Guys	More for Girls
Outdoor activities (like camping and fishing)		
Reading books		
Yoga or fitness classes		
Woodworking or building/fixing stuff		
Community service and volunteering		
Sewing, knitting, or other crafts		

The answers can be found in appendix D. The more you got right, the more you're familiar with society's activity expectations for guys and girls, regardless of whether you agree with them or not. Interestingly, and as you may have noted, while school, in general, is devalued for boys, there are certain courses (like science and math) that are associated more with boys and that don't elicit as much teasing when boys more actively engage and do well in them. Additionally, in general, teen guys have less "approved" activity options available to them than girls.

Now, please take a moment to reflect on the activities you circled, which represent those that you're into and those you're curious about, along with the items you didn't circle because they aren't of interest. Do your interests generally fall in the "More for Guys" or "More for Girls" categories, or are your interests split fairly evenly in both?

Going Deeper

So, why do you do what you do? This might feel like a weird question, or one with an obvious answer, but guys actually have all sorts of different reasons for doing what they do, including:

- (F) Wanting to *fit* in
- (G) *Genuine* enjoyment
- (P) Feeling *pressured* by parents or caregivers

- (E) *Expectations of society and the Guy Code*

- (O) *Some other reason*

Please return to the previous activity and code the things that you do or are curious about with the above categories; it's fine to use multiple codes per item when applicable. For instance, a guy could genuinely enjoy doing something (G), while also feeling pressured by his parents (P) to do that thing.

The codes can help you determine whether you do things more for yourself or in response to societal pressures. For instance, *E*'s are indicative of societal pressure, whereas *G*'s suggest you stand more on your own. No judgment either way. My responses as a teen would have included lots of *F*'s, some *G*'s and *E*'s, and no *P*'s. The goal of this exercise is to become more aware of when you're doing stuff that's in line with what you're *all about* versus due to outside influence from others.

Do Boys Feel Welcome in School?

Do you, in general, feel welcome at school? How about other guys you know?

Guys have a range of feelings about school, from "It sucks" to "It's tolerable" to "I enjoy it." Unfortunately, in addition to Guy Code messages that frame learning and academics as "unmanly" (Liang et al. 2019), other societal realities can send many guys the message that school is not the place for them:

- Starting as early as prekindergarten and continuing through twelfth grade, boys as a group get in trouble at much higher rates than girls, and boys of color even more so. That's no fun. The discipline isn't always fair, and that unfairness can be the result of discrimination. Boys can also be disciplined more harshly for doing the same things girls do (Owens 2016).

- There are fewer male teachers than female teachers, especially in public schools. And by "fewer," I mean not many at all. There are even fewer male teachers of color. What's up with that? Well, because society categorizes certain professions as being more for guys (for example, law, business, farming, and building and fixing stuff) or more for women (for example, nursing, teaching, and childcare), people often respond accordingly when picking careers. In most schools, the reality of not seeing male teachers at the front of most classrooms can reinforce the idea that school is not a place for us guys.

Can you think of other reasons why some boys, whether yourself or other guys, experience school as unfriendly and a less-welcoming place than it is for girls?

To keep it real, here are some of the school-based outcomes for guys, in general, compared to those of girls (Institute of Education Sciences 2021):

- We don't perform as well in any of the major subjects.

- We experience more time-outs, detentions, suspensions, and expulsions.

- We graduate from high school at lower rates.

- We go to college at lower rates.

Due to inequity and discrimination, all of these issues are worse for boys of color and boys from lower-income households (Ferguson 2016). The challenges many guys experience in school can contribute to all sorts of long-term life issues, including higher incarceration rates, lower-paying jobs and poverty, poor overall health, and elevated daily stress (Shollenberger 2015).

I'm not trying to be a downer by sharing all this information, but I want you to have the full picture. School is pretty serious business with how it impacts our lives. The last thing I want is for any guy to realize, once it's too late, that he should have taken school more seriously.

So, we are put in a tough situation when it comes to school and academics. Society pressures us guys to focus on achieving in sports, while it devalues the importance of school. Additionally, as noted above, school systems often don't do a great job of helping guys feel welcome. Yet we all have to go to school, five days a week, from the time we are five until we're eighteen years old. Furthermore, school performance can have heavy-duty consequences on our future and well-being.

Luis, a tenth-grader: I mean [fitting in] can lead you to stop socializing with certain people, just because other people might see him as uncool. Or, maybe you stop focusing on school because people see that as "Whatever," and you just wanna be the coolest kid, the toughest, the one that everybody wants to be like. And then I guess you lose—you lose everything that's going for you. And then you lose a little bit of yourself.

With his powerful words, Luis presents a dilemma and bind that many of us guys experience: wanting badly to fit in, and the consequences that can result from buying into this masculinity pressure. As he notes, "You lose a little bit of yourself." Have you ever felt like you lost a bit of yourself by trying to fit in, whether you stopped trying at school or changed yourself in some other way?

ACTIVITY 29: School and Your Future—Match or Mismatch?

School is a complicated space for many guys due to Guy Code pressures. This reality can have longer-term implications for the well-being and quality of life for many of us.

This activity will support you as you make sure your own approach to school aligns with your goals for the future. To begin, as much as any teen guy can know, please answer "yes," "no," or "kind of" for whether each "future goal" is one you care about now or likely will care about in the future. There are also two blank spaces for you to write in additional future goals of your own. Then, with each goal in mind, consider whether you work hard enough at school now in order to help yourself achieve this goal, and answer "yes," "no," or "kind of." The last column considers whether or not doing well in school is generally important for achieving the goal, at least according to societal norms. Just a reminder: this is all about you and how you want to be, so no pressure.

Future Goal	Is This Goal Something I Care About?	Am I Working Hard Enough for This Goal?	Is Doing Well in School Important for This Goal?
A specific career interest	Yes | No | Kind of	Yes | No | Kind of	Depends on career
Make pretty good money	Yes | No | Kind of	Yes | No | Kind of	Usually
Do well academically	Yes | No | Kind of	Yes | No | Kind of	Yes
Graduate from high school	Yes | No | Kind of	Yes | No | Kind of	Usually
Go to college or beyond	Yes | No | Kind of	Yes | No | Kind of	Usually
Want good career options	Yes | No | Kind of	Yes | No | Kind of	Usually
Financially support a family	Yes | No | Kind of	Yes | No | Kind of	Usually
	Yes | No | Kind of	Yes | No | Kind of	
	Yes | No | Kind of	Yes | No | Kind of	

Now, compare each of your "Is this goal something I care about?" responses to your "Am I working hard enough for this goal?" responses to establish whether you have a match or a mismatch. A mismatch happens when you report caring about the goal but aren't putting in enough effort at school to help yourself achieve it. Here's an example:

Gunther, a ninth-grader, *has the goal to "make pretty good money." He responded "kind of" for "Am I working hard enough for this goal?" This creates a mismatch in that Gunther cares about making pretty good money, which "usually" requires doing well in school, yet he isn't putting in the effort at school to help himself achieve the goal.*

Once you've assessed your responses, you'll have a sense for whether your future goals match up with the level of effort you're putting in at school. A mismatch indicates that you should assess your effort and consider upping it. This could include reaching out to someone you trust for support, such as a caregiver, a school counselor, or a teacher, if your performance in any classes is inadequate. For pretty much all of the goals listed, doing well in school is *usually* important.

Going Deeper

I worry about boys who don't try in school because it really can impact and limit their future, from making money to having a more meaningful job. It's unfortunate, but some guys realize too late, such as during senior year, that school performance actually matters to their future, and that it might be too late to turn their academic career around.

If you happen to be thinking *Sure, I had some mismatches in the above activity, but I don't want to get made fun of if I start working hard,* here are three ways you might approach putting in more effort at school.

The "own it" approach: I'm sure you know some guys who *own* being into school and working hard, even if they get teased about it, or worse. So, while not an easy choice to make in light of the Guy Code, some guys decide *This is who I am, and if you've got a problem with that, that's on you.* Of course, guys who follow this path need to be ready for some teasing, so here are some comebacks in case you take this approach:

- "Gotta be here every day; might as well make something of it."

- "I'm not gonna just throw away my time in here. I'm going places."

- "There's money on the line with my future."

- "Why are you worried so much about me and what I'm doing?"

You can probably come up with even better comebacks.

The street-cred approach: Guys who excel in a core Guy Code area can more easily get away with working hard in school. For example, if you're really good at sports, you probably won't get teased about putting in effort at school the way other guys might be, because you've already got pretty good *masculinity street credibility* built up. By the way, I'm not encouraging anyone to pretend to be something they're not to fit in. So, this approach will only work for those guys who already have the necessary street cred (which wouldn't have been me in high school).

The down-low approach: There are plenty of guys who decide that it's important to work hard in school, yet they want to do it on the down low. This approach doesn't create an easy or ideal learning situation, so here are two strategies you might use if you choose it:

- Set up extra help sessions with teachers after school or over the phone or online (if possible) in order to be more covert.

- Don't talk with guys you don't trust about your commitment to school, and stick to more standard "guy topics" when you're in a group.

Working toward future goals on the down low is not an easy situation to find yourself in; however, if you don't want to compromise your future, and the first two approaches don't feel like fits, being more covert about academics may be the right path for you.

Can't Win All the Time

While plenty of guys aren't into sports, lots are. There are many positives associated with playing sports, such as developing teamwork skills, mental toughness, and fitness, but, most importantly, sports are fun.

I was really into tennis while growing up. It was my main sport for a while, and I even went to a sleepaway tennis camp. Of course, some guys made fun of me for playing tennis because it's not as "tough" as other sports, but I really enjoyed it and had natural ability. So I dealt with the teasing and played. Sports like tennis, where it's just you and the opponent, provide unique lessons in mental toughness that differ from those related to team sports; for example, when you have an off day playing basketball, you can count on teammates to help out. In a sport like tennis, it's just you. All sports have unique lessons to provide, even if you don't consider yourself an athlete.

In spite of the many positives related to sports, most of us would probably agree that sports can have downsides. When taken to an extreme, sports can contribute to a number of issues for guys; for example, the sport can become something that feels more like a job and isn't fun anymore, guys can develop a bad attitude or be a sore loser, and guys can end up feeling really down or anxious during periods of lower performance. For example, I can remember getting really intense about JV soccer in high school. Seriously, it really mattered to me. I lost it a few times during games and got *really* physical with other players, which led to penalties, a pissed-off coach, and me getting benched until I learned to manage my emotions more effectively. With the considerable importance that society places on guys participating in and excelling at sports, it's easy for us to experience these and other negative consequences when we compete.

> **STOP AND THINK** *Can you think of any times when sports had a negative influence on you or didn't bring out your best? What happened?*

Let's take a closer look at the pressure guys experience to play sports, and how this pressure sometimes leads to problems.

ACTIVITY 30: When Pressure to Play Creates Problems

Here are some examples of tough situations guys can encounter with sports. Can you relate to any of these for yourself, and what advice would you give Alden, Jones, and Vishal if they were friends or teammates?

Alden, a seventh-grader, *is the best soccer player in his middle school. He's been playing soccer since he was five. Soccer is a pretty big deal in his family; his dad played professionally, and his sister got a full athletic scholarship and played in college. Alden doesn't remember ever being asked if he wanted to play; soccer is just kind of a family thing. The problem is he's starting to not enjoy it very much, especially because his dad now wants him to participate in indoor soccer in the winter instead of basketball, which he loves.*

What should Alden do?

Jones, a ninth-grader, *doesn't like sports and never has. While he didn't typically get picked last in gym class, he was usually pretty close, which hurt. Jones has an older brother and older sister who are into sports and have tried to get him involved, but he realized at a young age that he prefers doing other stuff. For instance, he really enjoys art and is a natural at painting. He's also a really skilled photographer and likes hiking and being in the outdoors. Jones also does pretty well academically. Because of his nonsports interests, Jones has been picked on and teased a lot and is feeling nervous about freshman year.*

What should Jones do?

Vishal, a twelfth-grader, *is really good at basketball. He loves it, and it's what he wants to be doing all the time. He also appreciates that it gives him status. Because he's on the varsity team, he gets invited to all the parties. Vishal was a perfectly fine student in middle school and got* Bs *and* Cs, *and he could get away with not putting in much effort. The problem is classes have gotten harder in high school, and he is in danger of failing two classes, which would mean that he would lose his place on the basketball team.*

What should Vishal do?

Going Deeper

As noted, there can be downsides to the pressure guys face to be into and good at sports. Please circle any you've experienced:

- Sports are no longer fun.

- Some guys really struggle with losing, and they trash themselves for having off days even though they're inevitable.

- Non-sports-related talents and skills are devalued, and the guys who have them are left out of certain activities and groups.

- Guys miss out on trying other activities because they're worried about being teased, or because the activities aren't valued by friends and family.

- School is devalued (as we explored).

- Some guys feel so much pressure to perform well and win that they take illegal drugs to get stronger (for example, steroids) or struggle with eating disorders (Eichstadt et al. 2020).

For any examples you circled, try to come up with a possible solution for yourself, and consider whether or not it makes sense to take positive action to deal with the issue. For example, some guys will need to have a talk with a parent who's living out their Olympic dreams through them. Don't laugh! This happens.

What's Your Take?

Good job sticking with this exploration of Guy Code Rule Number Five. You got to think more deeply about the pressure guys experience to play sports and not work hard at school, as well as some of the consequences. So, let's see where you stand.

ACTIVITY 31: Rule Number Five and You

At this point in the journey, do you think that pressure to play sports while taking other things less seriously, like school, is an issue for you or other guys? Why or why not?

- In particular, consider how this rule has worked for you and how you want to be.

- If you have mixed feelings, please identify the pros and cons of following this rule, both for you and other guys.

_____

_____

_____

_____

_____

_____

_____

_____

_____

_____

Moving On

So, that's it for Guy Code Rule Number Five for now. In this chapter you spent time thinking more deeply about your interests and exploring the influences underlying why you do what you do as it relates to sports, academics, and other stuff. For some guys this exploration will lead to straightforward conclusions; for example, they love sports, which is why they play them. Other guys may draw more complicated conclusions, such as realizing they play sports more for other people or don't try in school due to social pressure. Having worked through this chapter, I hope you'll be better equipped to do more of the stuff you really love and are curious about, whatever that means for you. Now, on to Guy Code Rule Number Six!

Chapter 7

Rule Number Six

Guys Shouldn't Be Like Those "Other" Groups

At its core, the Guy Code's about fitting in, and when teen boys don't follow the rules, they hear about it. Through living up to the various masculinity expectations we've explored so far, such as toughness, emotional control, and calling the shots, teen boys are able to prove that they belong (at least temporarily), while avoiding the ultimate threat of being called "a girl," "gay," or something similar. So, with any of the rules we've explored, the importance of toughness being an example, it isn't just about guys proving that they are sufficiently tough, but also about proving that toughness as a way to distance themselves from being compared to or associated with those "other" groups, namely girls and gay people.

In lots of ways, this final rule is the heart of the Guy Code and the ultimate expectation and pressure placed on us guys: *Don't act "feminine" or "gay," and prove that you aren't "one of them," and you'll be accepted as a "proper guy."* It also encompasses the other Guy Code Rules, because for guys to adequately distance themselves from these "other" groups, they must demonstrate adequate emotional control, toughness, sexual success with girls, the ability to call the shots, and the ability to excel at the "right activities," namely sports.

This is complicated stuff, and at this point, what's your sense of why the Guy Code takes such issue with girls and gay people? How do you personally feel about this anti-girl and anti-gay stance (which could be anything from "No big deal" to "Not cool")?

One of the primary ways that guys are reminded of expectations to distance themselves from these "other" groups—and are reprimanded and punished when they fail to behave accordingly—is through insults like "You're a girl," used by younger guys, to the more explicit "That's so gay" and "Don't be a pussy," used by teen guys as they get older. (This is also called "policing of masculinity" (POM); see chapter 1 for a refresher).

It's pretty much impossible to be a guy and not have anti-gay or anti-female insults directed at you, at least sometimes, whether you're the captain of the chess team or the starting quarterback. No guy can meet masculinity expectations all of the time, even for guys who want to and try really hard to do so. There will inevitably be slipups or times when you have to let your guard down. So, as this rule dictates, when guys act in ways that others perceive to be unmasculine and as associated with these *other* "lower-status" groups, they often get reprimanded through anti-gay and anti-female insults, and, consequently, reminded of Guy Code expectations. In this chapter I'll also use the term *accusations of otherness* for these types of insults.

How many times have you heard someone called something like "pussy" or "bitch" or been told to not be "gay"? How many times have words like this been directed at you? Most teen guys won't be able to provide a number because these insults are used so often. In my teen years, I heard them most days at school or while playing sports, directed at me and at other guys, whether used in a joking way or to be mean. How about you?

Words of Guys

Sammie, a twelfth-grader: I guess, like, sexist and maybe, uh, yeah, sexist jokes, sexist comments, or, like, comments about homosexuality are more, like—at least at [school]—they're like the major ways to communicate with one another.

Marco, a tenth-grader: Just don't take anything all personal because that's basically how they talk every day. If I say "faggot" and I offend somebody, like, I'm sorry, but it's just something that my friends use and something that I eventually picked up that I'm not proud of, but, um, if you're around it every day, you're eventually going to pick it up.

Sammie and Marco both discuss how insults are used frequently and generally are not taken too seriously, at least within their friend groups. Is this how it is at your school and with the guys you hang out with, or is it different? If so, how?

So, why do guys experience pressure to distance themselves from and reject things perceived as "feminine" or "gay," and where does this rule come from? I'll do my best to avoid turning this into a major history lesson, but here are two key explanations:

- In most parts of the world, women and gay people have historically (and currently) had less status and faced discrimination, while heterosexual boys and men (in general) have experienced more power and privilege. One of the ways that groups in power stay in power is by treating lower-status groups as inferior and less worthy. When guys use insults like "Don't be gay" or "Don't be a pussy," they are communicating that guys are better than those "other" groups, and that they shouldn't be like them or there will be consequences, like losing your place in "Guyland" (Kimmel 2008). These specific types of insults go back decades; in fact, my dad and his friends used them in the 1960s.

- The pressure guys experience to distance themselves from girls and gay people, fueled by accusations of otherness, also serves as a reaction to lower-status groups starting to get more social power. In response to girls/women and gay people demanding and receiving more rights and recognition in the twentieth-century, boys and men began to experience more pressure to prove their "superiority" over these "other" groups, such as by developing bigger muscles, exhibiting more toughness, and showing less emotion (Smiler 2019). Thus, these specific pressures and accompanying insults serve to remind boys and men to distance themselves from these "other" groups by sticking together, "staying strong," and continuing to call the shots.

So as you can see, and maybe had a sense of before, the pressure guys experience to distance themselves from things perceived as feminine or gay is complicated and deeply steeped within patriarchal (male-dominated) social structures. Furthermore, the insults that get used as a result of this pressure can be hurtful and are demeaning to girls and gay people, even if that's not the intention. You'll have the chance to explore these issues for yourself in this chapter, so let's take a closer look.

ACTIVITY 32: Accusations of Otherness Memory Jog

To start our exploration of the pressure us guys experience to distance ourselves from things perceived as "feminine" and "gay," I'd like you to reflect on some of your experiences of being pressured in these ways, including your exposure to *accusations of otherness*. The goal here is simply to get in touch with past memories and notice any feelings that show up (adapted from Reigeluth & Addis, 2021).

How often do you hear insults like "That's so gay," "Don't be a bitch," or something similar? Please circle one:

Never   Rarely   Few times a month   Few times a week   Daily

How old were you when you first heard insults like "That's so gay," "Don't be a bitch," or something similar directed at you? _____ Please take a moment to reflect on the situation, what was said, and what it felt like hearing those insults (confusing, upsetting, funny, or something else).

When was the most recent time you heard these types of insults directed at you?

_____

Please take a moment to reflect on the situation, what was said, and what it felt like.

Have you ever used insults like these (please circle one: Yes/No)? (Most of us guys will have, whether occasionally or frequently.) If yes, please circle the reasons why you've used those insults:

To be mean   To elevate myself   Just joking around

To remind guys of expectations   Something else

When you reflect on the most memorable time you witnessed other people being pressured to distance themselves from behaviors perceived as "feminine" or "gay," what was the "problematic" behavior getting called out, and how did you feel about the situation?

_____

_____

_____

When you reflect on the most memorable time you were pressured to distance yourself from behaviors perceived as "feminine" or "gay," what was the "problematic" behavior getting called out, and how did you feel as the recipient?

_____

_____

_____

When I think back on my experiences of being pressured to distance myself from these "other" groups, and of hearing these types of insults, I recall all different reactions, from laughter to feeling upset. This stuff is complicated. I certainly was never asked to do an activity like this as a teen guy, so nice work sticking with it.

Going Deeper

Guys frequently receive messages about the importance of acting in ways that won't be perceived as "feminine" or "gay" from friends and older guys, although some are also exposed to these "teachings" by family members, such as dads, older brothers, or uncles. Please reflect on the following:

- Have your male caregivers and family members, or family members of other genders, tried to convey that it's important for boys and men to distance themselves from behaviors perceived as "feminine" or "gay"?

- If so, what are some specific ways they've communicated this to you, whether through the standard insults or in some other way?

If you haven't had a conversation with your parents or caregivers about the pressure guys experience to prove their manhood by distancing themselves from behaviors perceived as "feminine" or "gay," consider asking them their thoughts: Were you exposed to similar messages growing up? What do you make of them? You might even ask them if they're surprised that many guys still use anti-gay and anti-female insults as a form of teasing and joking. Not all parents and caregivers share much about how things were for them growing up. It can be interesting and useful to get their take, and to also learn more about them when they were your age.

This Rule Makes It Harder to Be Close

A consequence of the Guy Code and this rule in particular (which I noted in chapters 1 and 2) is that many teen guys don't feel as emotionally close and connected to their guy friends as they would like. Simply put, emotional closeness requires making yourself vulnerable, at least sometimes—something that society characterizes as "feminine" behavior. Thus, many teen boys don't emotionally connect with their guy friends in more self-revealing and vulnerable ways, especially as they get older (Kindlon and Thompson 1999; Way 2011). However, they do find other ways to connect, such as through joking and doing activities together.

As noted, one of the common ways many teen guys joke around (and also bond) is by pressuring one another to be more masculine and to avoid behaviors perceived as "feminine" and "gay" (Oransky and Fisher 2009; Siebel Newsom 2015).

Words of Guys

Eduardo, a twelfth-grader, reflects on using insults like "That's so gay" and "You're a bitch" with his friends:

I think it depends on the person and if you're friends. Obviously, you don't do that to a random guy; you do it to somebody you're close to… I think in some ways it builds a bond. Because if you can do that with a friend, and they can do it back, and you don't get hurt, you have a bond there. (Reigeluth and Addis 2016, 19)

Can you relate to what Eduardo describes here, that using these types of insults in a back-and-forth way can build trust and help guys to feel closer? If yes, how so?

While I don't support the use of the insults we've been discussing, which I'll get into more later, I still enjoy joking around with my friends, engaging in playful teasing, and giving each other a hard time.

When teen boys rely on joking and teasing as their primary way to bond and connect, it often leads them to feel more distant in their friendships. This distance is, in large part, due to teen guys feeling worried that if they talk about more sensitive and vulnerable topics, they'll be accused of being "feminine" or "gay" and open themselves up to the whole range of anti-female and anti-gay insults. Even when delivered in a "just joking" kind of way, these insults make it harder for many guys to be more real with their friends. It often feels like the next put-down could come at any time—so, why risk opening up?

ACTIVITY 33: Ways You Connect

In spite of the pressure us guys experience to distance ourselves from things perceived as "feminine" or "gay," we have the potential to connect with our friends and other guys in all sorts of ways, including those listed in the following table.

Please take a moment to consider how you connect with friends and other guys, and whether or not you feel satisfied with the closeness of these relationships. Then, in the table, determine whether or not each way of connecting is relevant for you and your guy friends with a "yes," "no," or "kind of." You can use the blank spaces to write in any other ways that guys connect that I overlooked. Then, for the ways that are relevant for you (those for which you answered "yes" or "kind of"), please write down how they help you feel connected. If you have close friends who identify with other genders, please keep them in mind as well when completing this activity. To get you started, I included examples from Deshawn, an eleventh-grader.

Ways Guys Connect	Relevant for You? (Yes/No/Kind of)	How Does It Help You Feel More Connected?
Joking around using insults like "That's so gay," "Don't be a pussy," or something similar	Yes	Because they're funny; it's fun to laugh together, and not responding to them negatively shows others that you can handle it.
Playing sports together and being on the same team	Yes	You grow closer from battling and being on the same team.
Sharing secrets that other people don't know about	Yes	I only go here with a few close friends.
Talking about worries	Yes	It's helpful to not be on my own with stuff and to have a few guys I really trust.

Ways Guys Connect	Relevant for You? (Yes/No/Kind of)	How Does It Help You Feel More Connected?
Joking around using insults like "That's so gay," "Don't be a pussy," or something similar		
Joking around in other ways		
Roughhousing and wrestling		

Ways Guys Connect	Relevant for You? (Yes/No/Kind of)	How Does It Help You Feel More Connected?
Studying and doing homework		
Playing sports together and being on the same team		
Being part of the same club		
Playing video games		
Daring and challenging one another to do something		
Hugs or other physical forms of connecting, like arms around one another's shoulders		
Sharing secrets that other people don't know about		
Talking about feelings that you don't share with other people		
Talking about worries		

Ways Guys Connect	Relevant for You? (Yes/No/Kind of)	How Does It Help You Feel More Connected?

The more ways you endorsed, the more you and your friends have different ways of being close and showing that you care. If all of your "yes" and "kind of" responses were above the bold line, that's an indication that your friendships are more activity focused with less emphasis on discussing personal stuff, which could be influenced by Guy Code Rule Number Six and might be something worth considering further. Some guys are fine with this level of closeness, whereas others would prefer to feel emotionally closer to their friends, even though society considers this type of intimate and vulnerable sharing to be "feminine."

Going Deeper

Interestingly, the phrase "No homo" is one of the ways some guys show that they want to be closer with other guys, to bend the Guy Code, and to have more options for how to be. Of course, not all guys use this phrase. It wasn't in circulation when I was a teen. Have you ever used this phrase? If so, when and why?

Essentially, guys utter this phrase as a way to temporarily stray from masculinity expectations. Here are some examples: "No homo, but…"

- I really like Taylor Swift's new song. [Giving yourself permission to like a type of music that's more associated with girls]

- That shirt looks good. [Giving yourself permission to compliment a guy's appearance, which is a Guy Code no-no and perceived as a "feminine" thing to do]

- That movie made me cry. [Giving yourself permission to show vulnerable emotions, which society considers to be more of a "feminine" behavior]

There are lots of things guys might want to share with their friends to feel more connected and like they know one another better, including the examples above. But it can be hard to step beyond the Guy Code pressures to do so. If you want to be more connected to friends and talk more openly, including about difficult stuff, but struggle to figure out how to do so, here are a few tips:

- Do your best to become closer friends with people you can trust.

- Take some risks and let your closer friends in on worries and the tough stuff that's happening in your life.

- When you ask your friends how they're doing, if they try to brush it off, try digging a little deeper.

- If a friend seems like they're struggling, let them know that you're concerned and available to talk whenever they want.

Do you already do these things with close friends? If not, do you want to try any of them out? If yes, go ahead and circle those you'd like to try.

The Pressure to Distance Ourselves Can Really Hurt

Most teen guys will experience pressure to distance themselves from those "other" groups by being accused of "inappropriate" behavior considered "feminine" or "gay." While these moments can feel playful, they can also lead to hurt feelings and self-doubt (which I can certainly relate to).

 Do you feel like the pressure teen guys experience to distance themselves from things perceived as "feminine" or "gay" can ever go too far and can feel hurtful? What's the line for you, if there is one?

For example, I remember a time I was play-wrestling with a guy named Jordan in high school. Initially it felt fun. Other guys were watching and laughing. However, it became not fun when Jordan, who was bigger than me, pinned me on my back, with both of his legs around my chest, and started calling me "a bitch" and "a pussy." "Get the fuck off me," I told him. "You're not funny." He didn't get off me for a while. I felt powerless. Other guys laughed, which made the whole scene much worse. Jordan finally got up, laughing, and called me a "spaz." I told him he was "an asshole" and stormed off super pissed, and also hurt. Obviously, in this painful moment, Jordan demonstrated his physical superiority over me, while using accusations of otherness to make me feel less worthy.

I also remember a guy in middle school and high school, Devon, who got it the worst because he really struggled to demonstrate that he wasn't like those "other" groups. Guys were relentless, and I even chimed in at times, wanting to keep the negative attention as far away from me as possible. While Devon didn't really meet any of the standard masculinity markers, he was really nice and not looking to mess with anyone. I still feel bad that I didn't stand up for him.

> **STOP AND THINK** *Are there any guys at your school who get it the worst (which could include you)? What's your relationship like with those guys, and do you have any advice for them?*

The teen guys I've talked to about this stuff have provided me with many examples of how they feel and react when accusations of otherness, such as being called "a girl," "gay," or something similar, are hurtful and cross the line. These accusations make you:

- Feel like other guys think less of you

- Feel like you're not as good as other guys

- Question who you are

- Wonder *What if they really think I'm that way?*

- Second-guess yourself

- Behave more carefully and change something about yourself, so you don't get made fun of

Have you ever experienced any of these reactions? If so, which ones stand out, and why?

When I asked teen boys about accusations of otherness and whether using insults like "That's so gay," "Don't be a pussy," or something similar is a problem, they provided mixed opinions (Reigeluth and Addis 2016):

- Some feel like it's no big deal.

- Others reported that sometimes such insults are a problem and can be hurtful.

- A third group described feeling troubled and upset by these insults and believe they are a problem.

Are you surprised that guys are so mixed on this issue? What do you think?

ACTIVITY 34: Goes Too Far When…

For the teen guys who do think the pressures boys experience to prove their manhood and distance themselves from behaviors perceived as "feminine" and "gay" can be a problem, here are the feelings of some guys, in their own words, to consider, as well as follow-up questions:

Howie, a tenth-grader: *Like guys, I guess, think that they can play around with each other like that, and they think that because guys are supposed to be—made out to be strong and not show any signs of emotion, that nobody's going to care about it, and it doesn't hurt them. But what they don't know is that it really hurts people when they think about it, because they go home and they start to think about it, and they really doubt themselves… When you call a kid "a pussy" he kind of doubts himself physically and how he is masculine type, like how big he is or how strong he is… So, I guess it's just that the kids know that it hurts, because if they get called it then they know it hurts; that's why they try to use it.*

How do you feel about Howie's assessment of the ways these accusations can be hurtful and make guys "doubt themselves"? Have you ever experienced anything like that yourself?

Javier, a tenth-grader: *So, I was questioned that day, like, um, "Are you sure—like, you're not gay? I mean, like, it's okay, but just making sure I don't want to make any messed-up jokes around you"... Well, like, it was just the fact that they have known me for so long and think I'm suddenly gay—kind of, made me feel a little upset. But, I knew it was just joking for one day, so I didn't really mind it that day; I just continued my day how I normally would.*

So, Javier says he "didn't really mind it" when his friends asked if he was "gay." Do you buy it? If not, how do you think he was really feeling?

Joe, a twelfth-grader: *I feel like there's probably, like, a quarter of guys in my grade are pretty against that stuff, but I feel like a lot of them wouldn't even say anything, you know what I mean? Like, they'll even say it just to go with that trend, you know?... I know that there are, like, some things that need to change, and I try. I don't like to hear people saying derogatory things. Like, it makes someone feel inferior. It's really messed up.*

I can definitely relate to Joe's words about the pressure to just "go with that trend." How about you? What makes it so hard for guys who experience these insults as derogatory and hurtful to take a stand?

Going Deeper

We've all been in situations where someone said something—pressuring us to be more masculine or punishing us for behaving in a way perceived as "feminine" or "gay"—that felt mean and not right, whether directed at us or other guys. Those can be tough moments that lead to bad feelings and thoughts like *Do I say something? Should I stand up for myself? Should I defend that other guy? I want to say something, but I also don't want to get ripped on.* When was the last time you were in this type of situation? What happened, and how did you feel about the outcome?

Not only do these situations feel bad, but most of us don't feel good if we don't say anything. If you ever find yourself wanting to take a stand, but understandably feel overwhelmed or don't know how, here are some possible ways to let other guys know you aren't down with what they said:

- "It's not cool to say things like that, and it's insulting to gay people [or girls and women]."

- "Can't you come up with something a little more creative? That's so 1990s, bruh."

- "What's your problem with gay people [or girls and women]?"

- "Times have changed, man. It's not cool to say that stuff anymore."

- "That's just mean. What's your deal? Oh yeah, insecurity."

- "Wow, you must be having a really bad day."

Feel free to circle any examples you could see yourself using, and write in your own possible responses here.

_____

_____

_____

_____

Of course, any time we take a stand, it's important to try to be mentally ready for potential fallout, which could be other guys coming after you with more insults, or even physically in extreme cases. Taking a stand is a decision for each of us to make individually.

Don't Be Like *Them*

Alright, now that we've unpacked topics related to the pressure that guys experience, and can put on one another, to prove that they aren't like girls and gay people, let's get into a key question at the heart of this Guy Code Rule: Do the boys and men who engage in the behaviors and insults we've been discussing have something against these "other" groups? Please take a moment to sit with that question and notice what comes up.

Of course, lots of guys defend the specific insults that get used to let guys know when their behaviors are out of line: "When we use these words, they aren't homophobic. I have nothing against gay people. They really just mean you aren't being manly." I understand where this argument comes from because I used these insults, and pressured other guys in these ways, when I was a teenager. I would have defended their use in the same way and was socialized to think that pressuring guys through accusations of otherness was okay. However, that was long before I received my own Guy Code and masculinity education and started to think about this stuff for myself.

Before we go further into this complicated, challenging, and likely uncomfortable topic, let me take a moment to provide simplified definitions of two important terms to make sure we're on the same page:

- *Homophobic:* For our purposes, this word refers to derogatory insults directed toward boys and men who identify as gay, bisexual, or queer. In general, this term refers to prejudice and negative attitudes directed toward these groups. Homophobic insults serve multiple purposes for the Guy Code and, consequently, guys. First, they reinforce the idea that to be gay is "bad" and something to be looked down upon. Second, they can be used as a threat to exclude guys who don't sufficiently prove themselves and their masculinity (by the users distancing themselves from these "other" groups).

- *Misogynistic:* For our purposes, this word refers to derogatory insults directed toward girls and women. In general, this term refers to prejudice and negative attitudes directed toward girls and women. Misogynistic insults reinforce the idea that girls and women are inferior and essentially communicate "Don't act like a girl, or we'll think less of you."

Alright, let's go deeper into this tricky topic of whether guys who use anti-gay and anti-female insults, and who pressure one another in these ways, are homophobic and misogynistic. I certainly wasn't asked to think about this complicated and likely uncomfortable topic when I was your age, so way to go for hanging in there.

ACTIVITY 35: **Are Most Guys Homophobic and Misogynistic?**

In consideration of the previous definitions for "homophobic" and "misogynistic," please answer the following questions. It would have been challenging for me to answer them at your age, so please just do your best. It's fine to answer in your head if that feels more comfortable.

Do you consider any of the guys you hang out with to be homophobic (that is, anti-gay) or misogynistic (that is, anti-female) in any way? Why or why not?

_____

_____

_____

_____

_____

Do you consider yourself to be homophobic or misogynistic in any way? Why or why not?

_____

_____

_____

_____

_____

For guys who acknowledge that they have some homophobic or misogynistic beliefs or ways of behaving (which I definitely did as a teen, and even in college), please know that answering these questions is not about making anyone feel bad, although it's important to notice this emotion if it's surfacing. This activity is about developing self-awareness; it's about recognizing that us guys are socialized within a system that rewards many of us with power while treating other groups, such as gay people and girls and women, as inferior. So, when it comes to their beliefs and behaviors, many guys will be *a little bit* to *a lot* homophobic and misogynistic. The question for you is, does that work for who you are and how you want to be?

Going Deeper

Alright, nice work hanging in there with those tough questions and this sensitive topic. If you feel like accusations of otherness rise to the level of being derogatory or hurtful toward girls and women and people who are gay or queer, and that using these types of insults isn't what you're about, here's an opportunity to commit to not using them. But first, a friendly reminder: There's no pressure from me at all regarding what you choose to do. This commitment is fully about you and whatever feels true to you. It's also cool if you want to modify the wording of the commitment to suit you.

So, here it is: *Do I want to try my best to not use these types of insults?* Please circle one:

I commit   **I'm good**   **Still considering**

If you end up committing and have some slipups along the way, please take it easy on yourself. Change is a process, and most teen guys have been exposed to homophobic and misogynistic insults since childhood. Their use runs deep in the Guy Code and is central to the pressure guys experience to distance themselves from things perceived as "feminine" and "gay."

What's Your Take?

Way to go! You directly faced and considered the pressure teen guys experience to distance themselves from those "other" groups, along with the insults that frequently accompany this pressure, like "That's so gay" and "Don't be a pussy." Most importantly, you got to reflect on your own experiences and feelings and how this rule has worked in your life. So, let's see where you stand.

ACTIVITY 36: **Rule Number Six and You**

Do you think that the pressure teen guys experience to distance themselves from these "other" groups, and specifically from the behaviors perceived as "feminine" or "gay," is an issue for you or other guys? Why or why not?

- In particular, consider how this rule has worked for you and how you want to be.

- If you have mixed feelings, please identify identity the pros and cons of this rule for you and other guys.

_____

_____

_____

_____

_____

_____

_____

_____

_____

_____

Moving On

Six down! Alright, you made it through all of the Guy Code Rules and have now had the chance to think more deeply about the core pressures us guys receive to be a certain way, including the ultimate rule of distancing ourselves from those "other" groups, specifically behaviors perceived as "feminine" or "gay." You've also thought about tricky issues that we aren't frequently encouraged to consider more critically and for ourselves, like whether the Guy Code contributes to guys endorsing homophobic and misogynistic attitudes. As you are hopefully well aware now (if not before), whether you follow all, certain parts, or none of the Guy Code is an individual decision for each one of us to make on our own terms. With that in mind, we'll now move on to the final two chapters that will support you as you think even more deeply about who you are and how you want to be as a guy and a person.

Part 3

Who You Are and Your Awakened Masculinity

Chapter 8

Guy Code x Culture x Identity

It would have been easier to write this book without going into the topic of culture. Discussing culture gets complicated quickly because it means very different things to different people, even to those who share cultural identities or have similar backgrounds. I know that the Guy Code and masculinity stuff are already pretty complicated topics, but I'd be doing you a disservice if we didn't take a look at how culture can influence guys and their understanding of and experience with the Guy Code. For instance, some guys have a harder time living up to Guy Code expectations because their cultural backgrounds and identities don't provide them with as much social status as other guys.

While most guys have heard the term "culture," it's not a topic we've all explored or thought about for ourselves. What about you? Please mark an X below to indicate how much you've thought about what "culture" means for you.

Not Much	Some	Lots

As we explore the topic of culture in this chapter, please keep in mind that some guys are very comfortable thinking about what it means for them, others less so. It's all good wherever you find yourself.

As a teen guy, I had essentially no experience thinking about culture. Within the white, heteronormative culture I lived in, it just wasn't discussed or mentioned. This is a common experience for people belonging to dominant and privileged social groups (Kimmel and Ferber 2017). By the way, I didn't hear or learn about the technical term "heteronormative" until college. It means growing up in communities in which heterosexuality is the clear preference, and in which there is less contact with sexual and gender minorities, such as people who identify with LGBTQ+ communities (see appendix B for an overview of some of these identities).

When the society you live in is run by people who look like you and share your different identities, it's easier to not think about culture that much, because when you look around you see things that represent you (Kimmel and Ferber 2017). In US and European contexts, some examples of this "representation" include:

- The majority of political leaders are white men.

- Most leading characters on TV and in movies are white.

- The majority of professional sports teams and companies are owned by white men.

What other examples can you think of? While some progress has been made to change and address these inequities (for example, minority groups having more media representation), US and European societies still have a long way to go to ensure that all people are treated as equals and given the same opportunities.

> **STOP AND THINK** *What does "culture" mean to you, and which of your identities come to mind as you consider that term?*

As an adult I've become much more aware of how culture has impacted me, including in regard to gender and the Guy Code. So, what is "culture"? *Culture* pertains to the unique practices, traditions, viewpoints, and experiences of a distinct group of people in a particular society (Howard 1991). Race—having to do with skin color and other physical characteristics—is commonly associated with culture, but there are other key categories that influence culture, including:

- Ethnicity (the cultural practices and traditions, including unique languages, clothing, and food, shared by groups of people from the same country or region)

- Religion

- Socioeconomic class (for example, lower, middle, and upper)

- Sexual orientation

- Gender

- Lifestyle (for example, rural versus urban)

Each of these cultural elements, or "identities," along with how they intersect, influences how we individually experience masculinity and the Guy Code, as well as ourselves in general. This list isn't exhaustive, and there are plenty of other cultural categories that can come into play, such as those based on specific activities (for example, "hippie culture," "gamer culture," "heavy metal culture," "military culture," and "football culture"). Do any additional examples come to mind for you?

Here is a *simplified* example and representation of the intersectionality of different cultural identities:

Ramon, a ninth-grader originally from Spain, *identifies with gamer culture. He comes from a working-class background, so his family has difficulty helping him buy the latest consoles and games. He works at a grocery store after school, while some of his guy friends who have more financial privilege spend their time gaming. Ramon loves gaming, even though he doesn't see many game characters who look like him. Because of his economic status, and the fact that he identifies with multiple minority and marginalized groups, he feels less powerful and less confident than some of his guy friends in town. He also doesn't have a fancy gaming system due to financial limitations.*

Hopefully, this snapshot helps you understand a little better how cultural identities can intersect and interact, and how they're reflected in one's experience of and relationship with the Guy Code. Due to his economic status, and the fact that Ramon identifies with cultural groups with less power, he has a harder time meeting some of the Guy Code expectations (to feel confident and call the shots) than some of his friends from more privileged and higher-status backgrounds.

In spite of the cultural diversity and differences we each possess, including our styles, interests, and ways of being, all guys have some shared life experiences and identities due to the pressures we receive to meet masculinity expectations and to prove our "manhood" (Gilmore 1990). From this common foundation, our genetics and differing life experiences, including the cultural groups we identify with, shape us uniquely. Thus, how we experience Guy Code pressures, and what we do in response to them, differs significantly. A term used to acknowledge the diverse ways of being a guy, as well as the layered diversity within the gender category of boys and men, is *masculinities* (Connell 2005).

Let's take a closer look at cultural identities and what they've meant for you.

ACTIVITY 37: **Defining Culture for Yourself**

Culture can be a very personal thing for each of us. Please take some time to reflect on what culture means to you.

Please identify your cultural and other identities that are most important to how you see yourself and what you're all about. For each identity, please briefly describe why it's important to you.

_____

_____

_____

_____

_____

Who has taught you about your cultural and other identities that are the most important to you (could be no one or someone really influential, like a grandparent, caregiver, friend, or even a famous person)? What feels most meaningful about the things you've learned from them?

_____

_____

_____

_____

_____

Going Deeper

Culture can start to feel more complicated when we begin to consider the different identities we have. A big term that gets used for this sort of exploration is *intersectionality*, which essentially refers to how cultural identities uniquely contribute to one's belief system and societal experience and make you who you are (Crenshaw 1991). If you aren't familiar with this term, no worries. I didn't learn about "intersectionality" until after high school, so you are ahead of me. Another way to think about this concept is that we each are a "cultural pot" full of a unique combination of ingredients.

So, how about exploring the intersectionality of your own cultural identities? Please consider each cultural identity (Hays 2016) included in the following table. Note how you identify for each, the identity's level of importance for you ("low," "medium," or "high"), and then briefly explain why you answered as you did. There are blank spaces for you to add other important identities I missed, if you want. It's also fine to do this activity in your head if that feels more comfortable. Here's an example from Marcus, an eighth-grader.

Cultural Identity	How You Identify	Level of Importance (Low, Medium, or High) and Why
Race and/or ethnicity	Biracial (Black and white)	High. Race matters, especially when you're biracial and Black.
Sexual orientation	Straight	Medium. I don't think about it much.
Where you were born and where you live	California	High. I've always lived here, and I'm into LA's teams.

Cultural Identity	How You Identify	Level of Importance (Low, Medium, or High) and Why
Race and/or ethnicity		
Socioeconomic status or class		

Religion		
Sexual orientation		
Ability/disability		
Gender		
Where you were born and where you live		

Great work. Please take a moment to notice what this activity felt like for you. Did any identities stand out either because of their importance or because you hadn't thought about them much before? Please circle any that influence how you experience the Guy Code, along with your unique identity as a guy.

When Culture and Privilege Meet the Guy Code

All of us guys have at least one thing in common: we all know what it feels like to be pressured to prove ourselves and to "man up," regardless of how we feel about this pressure. However, aside from this one shared experience, we're a pretty diverse group with regard to our dispositions, interests, styles of dress, and, of course, cultural backgrounds and intersectionality. Just look around.

Do you and your guy friends have similar or different cultural backgrounds? What about your interests?

Based on cultural backgrounds and different identities, guys also have varying levels of social status and privilege. What comes to mind when you hear the word "privilege"? Basically, *privilege* refers to the greater amount of power and advantage a person has in society due to appearance, family background, and cultural identities, like the ones listed in the exercise you just completed. When you have more privilege, it's easier to access the resources that can help you achieve the type of life you want. Here are some commonly recognized indications that one experiences privilege:

- Having more wealth, including making a lot of money or owning property

- Having access to training or educational opportunities that can lead to a more desirable job (as defined by the society one lives in)

- Seeing people who look like you in positions of power and represented in the media, in your community, and in society at large

- Having regular access to health care and medical services

- Experiencing the legal system and government as fair and representative of you and your interests

Do any other examples come to mind?

Based on your background and cultural identities, do you identify as having more or less privilege than others? Why?

Have you heard the term "marginalized" before? If so, what comes to mind when you hear it? A *marginalized* person is someone who's at a societal disadvantage. It's harder for them to get ahead because they're discriminated against and treated unfairly for not belonging to social groups that have power and privilege (Hays 2016). Some guys experience privilege due to some of their cultural identities, yet they are marginalized for others, such as for being gay or for coming from a working-class background. Other guys are marginalized due to most of their cultural identities, like being a guy of color from a lower-class background who also identifies as gay, bisexual, or trans.

Regardless of whether you identify with privileged or marginalized cultural groups and identities, cultural belonging has the potential to provide all people with advantages, including a sense of pride, belonging to something special and bigger than yourself, a shared experience, and feeling more understood by and connected to a community. Furthermore, just as the Guy Code isn't all-powerful when it comes to you and the way you are, cultural identities also don't dictate what we're all about. So, while it's a given that our cultural backgrounds will influence our life experiences, we all get to decide which of our identities are the most important to us.

Experts have studied boys and men from different racial and ethnic backgrounds and found that culture can influence their experience of being a guy and the messages they receive. Please keep in mind that each cultural background noted below is diverse and made up of lots of different types of guys. Thus, these findings will apply to some of the guys who identify with these specific cultural groups and not others.

- As a result of encountering threats connected to racism and inequality, Black boys and men experience heightened pressure to conceal vulnerable emotions and to appear tough and hardened (Majors and Billson 1993). Additional masculine norms that can be particularly important to Black boys and men include accountability, family, pride, and spirituality (Hunter and Davis 1992).

- American Indian and Alaskan Native boys can be taught to embrace both masculinity and femininity, which conflicts with dominant Guy Code culture (Rouse 2016).

- It's easier for white guys with more privilege to meet Guy Code expectations, especially calling the shots and having power over others, because they have more opportunities and access to financial and other resources (Kimmel and Ferber 2017).

- Two influential brands of masculinity have been identified for Latino/Hispanic boys and men. *Machismo,* also called "hypermasculinity," represents masculine norms taken to the extreme, whereas *caballerismo* emphasizes family values and caretaking (Mora 2012).

- East Asian boys and men are often stereotyped as being more "feminine" than guys from other cultural groups (Iwamoto and Kaya 2016). They must also contend with the "model minority myth" that stereotypes them as being more submissive and scholarly.

Can you relate to any of these findings?

ACTIVITY 38: Guys on the Margin

While it's impossible for any guy to fully meet the expectations of the Guy Code, as doing so would involve never feeling worried or insecure, among other requirements, some guys encounter more difficulty meeting expectations because they identify with a marginalized identity or background.

In the following table, you'll find some of the marginalized identities that can make it harder for someone to meet Guy Code pressures. The middle column includes the perspective of a guy who illustrates why it can be harder to meet certain masculinity expectations as a result of their identity (and belonging to that group). Your task is to reflect on whether you or someone you know identifies with any of these marginalized groups. If you identify and have personal experience with the group, please write *P* in the last column; if you know someone else who does, write a *K*. It's fine to answer in your head if that feels more comfortable. There are two additional rows at the bottom to write in other marginalized groups you'd like to include.

Marginalized Identity	Harder to Meet Guy Code Expectations Because Guys with This Identify Often...	Personal Experience (*P*) or Know Someone (*K*)
Gay, bisexual, or asexual (that is, not interested in sex or arousal)	Can't live up to the pressure guys experience to be hetero, a player, and highly sexually active with girls.	
Physical disability	Have a harder time excelling in more physically demanding sports even though plenty of guys with disabilities are excellent athletes. It's also more difficult to "call the shots" because of needing more assistance.	
Gender minority, such as trans man or transmasculine	Experience difficulty fitting in and being accepted by other guys, sometimes due to appearance or because other guys know they're trans, and they look down on that.	
Racial minority, such as boy or man of color	Experience not having status, and lack opportunities to call the shots the way many white guys do. Racism and discrimination make life tougher on a daily basis.	
Lacking ideal body type	Experience crap from other guys for being overweight and thus not meeting the "masculine ideal," which hurts.	
Lower socioeconomic background	Miss out on a lot of stuff other guys are able to do because of having to work to help family. Because it's harder to afford many things, these guys can feel like they have less status and power.	

Marginalized Identity	Harder to Meet Guy Code Expectations Because Guys with This Identify Often...	Personal Experience (**P**) or Know Someone (**K**)

While the Guy Code poses challenges for all boys and men, it's pretty clear that it's more difficult for some guys to meet expectations. How's it for you?

Going Deeper

Pretty much all of us guys, and people in general, have *cultural knowledge gaps*. What does that mean? Well, a cultural knowledge gap is a limited awareness and understanding of a certain cultural group. I've got plenty of cultural knowledge gaps myself. It's impossible to be a human and not have some, since none of us can know or have meaningful interactions with people of all cultural identities and backgrounds.

Cultural knowledge gaps become more problematic when they include *implicit biases* (less intentional and less conscious) and *explicit biases* (intentional and very conscious). As you may already know, a bias encompasses negative beliefs one has about a certain cultural group, and biases can lead to unfair and unjust behaviors being directed toward that group. For example, one Guy Code bias is that women are weaker and not as mentally tough as men, which has historically led to women not being offered certain jobs.

Please take a moment to reflect on your knowledge gaps, which we all have:

- Considering the cultural identities listed earlier in this chapter, determine which ones you have more or less experience with, along with any other groups that come to mind.

- Do you hold any negative views or stereotypes about any particular cultural identities (which can be common when one has less experience with certain groups)? Do you view any as being more favorable or less favorable? Do any of your caregivers have such views? Our caregivers can influence how we feel about different groups and cultural identities.

This is uncomfortable and difficult work to do. Biases are part of the human condition; they're a part of living in hierarchical societies with racism, oppression, privilege, and marginalization. If you'd like to have fewer biases and more self-awareness, difficult exercises like this can be helpful.

Bigger Stuff You Care About

Can you imagine asking an eight-year-old about their values, social issues like poverty or the environment, and whether they identify as liberal or conservative? You'd probably get a long stare, or lots of questions, and then chances are that eight-year-old would go back to playing. But for teenagers like you, it's expected and natural for you to start developing a clearer sense of your values and views that are part of your identity and what you're all about. This doesn't fully happen during your teens; it's a gradual process that can stretch into your twenties and beyond (Arnett 2018).

When you think about the most important parts of your identity, which includes your values, interests, and views, what things are most central to who you are and what you're all about?

So, what exactly are values? People frequently confuse them with goals, so let's take a look at both:

- *Goals* are shorter- or longer-term things that we can check off a list. Once they are checked off, they are done and that's that. Shorter-term goals include things like getting an A in a class and finding a date for a school dance. Longer-term goals, like graduating from high school or becoming the captain of a sports team or the president of a club, take more planning and preparation. What are some goals that you are working on right now?

- *Values* never get checked off a list, and you're always working on them. They give our lives direction. Some classic values include honesty, integrity, selflessness, compassion, empathy, resilience, and kindness. Why can't we check values off a list the way we can goals? Well, as soon as you do, you're not doing the value anymore, right? Take honesty, for example. If you ever stop working on being honest, then you're no longer an honest person, and that value goes away. During tough times, we can stray from our values and what we're all about, but we can always get back to them with hard work, if we want to.

Not surprisingly, the cultural groups we identify with frequently influence our values, so let's take a look at what that might mean for you.

ACTIVITY 39: My Cultural Identities and Values

Please write down up to five cultural identities that are important to you (if it might be helpful, see the examples provided earlier in the chapter). Then, take a moment to reflect on some of the cultural values connected to those different groups and write them in the second column. I provided an example to get you started. Next, reflect on your own personal values and write whatever comes to mind in the third column. If you struggle to come up with ideas, a quick internet search for "common values" will provide lots of options to consider. Lastly, circle any cultural values you aren't on board with, or that aren't that important to you, and consider whether that mismatch has led to any difficulties or stress. (For example, some cultural groups value "obedience to elders," which might present challenges for some teens striving to establish their own identity.)

My Cultural Identities	Some Core Values of This Identity	My Key Values
American Indian	Family and heritage	

Going Deeper

In the process of answering the questions "Who am I?" and "What am I all about?" (which includes determining individual values), teens like you start to become more independent and usually start to consider whether or not they agree with their parents or caregivers on different issues. Younger children don't really question their parents and caregivers in these ways, but teens typically do. Please take a moment to explore what's true for you by reflecting on the following questions:

- Have you thought much about whether you agree or disagree with your parents (or caregivers) on different issues or values?

- Are there specific issues or values that your parents (or caregivers) and you clearly agree or disagree on, such as ones involving conservative versus liberal viewpoints? If so, which ones and why?

- Do you and your parents (or caregivers) agree on issues relating to gender and gender identities, including those related to the Guy Code and societal expectations for teen boys? If you answered no, what views of yours differ from theirs?

- If you've ever disagreed with your parents (or caregivers) on an issue or value, what was that experience like? For some teen guys it's not a big deal, but for others it can be tough water to navigate, depending on the issue.

Great work thinking through all that. Determining one's values and beliefs about different issues can lead to disagreements in families, creating challenging dynamics with parents and caregivers. This process can be especially complicated for some teen guys.

Moving On

Alright, you're doing great! In this chapter you had the chance to think more deeply about your own cultural and group identities and how they've influenced you and affected your experience of being a guy. You also got to think about the diverse backgrounds of other guys, and how their lives can be different from yours based on their own cultural and group identities. These are complicated topics for us all, and it's pretty cool that you gave them some thought and hopefully got to know yourself better in the process. One more chapter to go!

Chapter 9

What Most Teen Guys Don't Hear: You Have Gender Choices

Way to go! It's pretty cool that you're nearing the end of this book and have made it this far in the journey. More often than not, we receive the not-so-subtle message to "Do this and be that" with regard to masculinity expectations. Society treats the Guy Code as a given, as dictating how we're supposed to be, rather than inviting us to decide for ourselves who we are and how we want to be as guys and human beings. You've now explored a lot of complex and tricky stuff that us guys aren't typically encouraged to think about for ourselves, including:

- Gender basics, along with the gender binary and the more expansive and fluid gender spectrum

- Gender socialization—that is, how you've been taught what it means to be a guy

- Guy Code messages and pressures related to how we should be regarding emotions, toughness, sexuality, calling the shots, interests, and distancing ourselves from "other" groups (namely girls and gay people) through our behaviors

- The reality that guys make up a diverse group of individuals with different styles, interests, skills, cultural backgrounds and identities, emotional dispositions, and ways of being in the world

> *As you reflect back on where you started this journey compared to where you are now, what stands out, especially with regard to your understanding of the Guy Code and how it's influenced you, whether positively, negatively, or both?*

We'll spend our remaining time together focused on exploring and making sense of where you are now and how you'd like to continue moving forward in your life, which brings us to *awakened masculinity*. I define "awakened masculinity" as having a greater awareness of how gender and the Guy Code work, and, consequently, having the opportunity to be more thoughtful and intentional in defining masculinity and gender for yourself. Awakened masculinity is not about allowing society to command or tell us how we should be. It's about guys having the opportunity to be fully educated about gender basics and the masculinity pressures they've encountered, and will continue to encounter, with the invitation to then decide who they are and how they want to be as guys and as people.

Let's take a closer look at what awakened masculinity means for you.

ACTIVITY 40: Awakened Masculinity and Me

Now that you've had a behind-the-scenes look at how the Guy Code operates, you've considered what parts of it work for you and what ones don't. So, let's take a closer look at where you've ended up with your takes on the different masculinity pressures that pretty much all guys experience.

For each rule listed below, please clarify whether it works for you with a "yes," "no," or "kind of." Then, briefly clarify what about that rule works or doesn't work for you. This activity is meant to be brief, since you already did more in-depth *What's Your Take* reflections to clarify your thoughts on each rule. You can refer back to these reflections at any time.

Guy Code Rule	Does It Work for You? (Yes/No/ Kind of)	Clarify in Your Own Words… What Works and What Doesn't?
#1. Guys should hide difficult emotions		
#2. Guys should be tough at all times		
#3. Guys should be players		
#4. Guys should call the shots and be alphas		
#5. Guys should play sports—school… not so much		
#6. Guys shouldn't be like those "other" groups		

Next, please review "Activity 1: Gender and Guy Code Self-Assessment," which you filled out in the book's introduction; "Activity 3: My Gender Identity and Expression" and the "Going Deeper" section that followed (on masculinity expectations and your identity); and the "Going Deeper" section after activity 5 (on being a role model for other guys). The responses you offered for these activities will collectively provide you with a sense of where you started the journey.

As you review these early responses, give some thought to whether anything has changed in relation to your responses above, including your overall understanding of gender, masculinity pressures, and what being a guy means to you. Some guys will experience and notice more change than others. Wherever you're at, it's all good. The important thing is that you've undertaken this journey and spent time thinking critically about the Guy Code and what feels right for you.

Going Deeper

Alright, you just had a chance to reflect on the different Guy Code Rules in your own words and to further solidify your take on them. When you think about what being a guy means to you, the things you care about, and your own values, what does the Guy Code lack that matters to you? From service to others to equality and justice to passion for cooking, the list of things not endorsed by the Guy Code that different guys still care about is endless. What are those things for you that make you uniquely who you are? The following prompt may be helpful:

In addition to my position on the various Guy Code Rules (noted in the above activity), other values and interests that are important to defining what being a guy means for me include:

_____

_____

_____

_____

_____

_____

_____

_____

How I Want to Be

At this point, you should have a pretty clear sense of which of the Guy Code Rules you're good with, and which ones don't work for who you are and how you want to be. For guys thinking about making some changes because certain aspects of the Guy Code aren't working for them, keep in mind that change, for any of us, is a process that takes time, trial and error, patience, and, hopefully, some sort of a plan. As we've explored, the masculinity pressures we experience are significant, and most guys start hearing messages like "Big boys don't cry" and "Don't be a girl" at a young age, so these socialization teachings can run deep.

 When was the last time there was something you wanted to get better at or improve about yourself? How do you typically approach self-growth, which we all need at times?

It can be confusing to know where and how to begin making changes. So, let's take a look at some strategies and skills that might be useful, depending on what type of change you're interested in. Even for guys feeling like *I'm good—all of the Guy Code Rules are working just fine,* please still check out these strategies and skills; you might find one or more that seems worth trying out.

ACTIVITY 41: Self-Growth Strategies and Skills

In the following table, circle each Guy Code Rule that you reported isn't fully working for you (by answering "no" or "kind of" in activity 40). For each circled rule, read through the associated possible "ways to change" and "self-growth skills" you might use to support change in that specific area, and circle any that seem like they might be worth trying out. I also included blank cells at the bottom in case you have other "ways to change" or "skills" you'd like to note. Even if you reported that all of the Guy Code Rules are working for you (by answering "yes" in activity 40), you may see a skill or two that seems like it could be useful. If so, circle them. As part of your own self-care, you may already be using some of the listed skills, which is awesome!

Rules	Ways to Change (You Decide)	Self-Growth Skills
#1. Guys should hide difficult emotions	Strengthening my emotional awareness	• Journal about how I'm feeling and what's going on internally • Support myself to experience the full range of emotions by using mindfulness skills (do an internet search for options to try)
	Supporting myself when I'm feeling uncertain or scared	• Talk to a trusted friend, mentor, or caregiver
#2. Guys should be tough at all times	Giving myself permission to not always have to be tough	• Create a mantra about the importance of "keeping it real and being safe," whatever that means for me • Review toughness pros and cons (see activity 14)
	Saying no when something feels unsafe or goes against my values	• Hold my ground (see the "Going Deeper" section after activity 15)
#3. Guys should be players	Being more open and transparent in sexual or romantic relationships	• Notice when I'm holding back (mindfulness can support this skill) • Practice initiating challenging conversations and sharing more openly (Just gotta do it) • Schedule regular time to talk about a relationship and how it's going
	Making asking for consent a regular thing I do	• Review the tips in the "Don't Forget Consent" section, and check out Smiler (2016) for a deeper dive

Rules	Ways to Change (You Decide)	Self-Growth Skills
#4. Guys should call the shots and be alphas	Becoming a more agreeable alpha	• Work on my listening and cooperation skills (see the "Going Deeper" section after activity 24)
	Asking for help when I need it	• Practice by starting with easier "asks" first, like "Can I borrow [that thing]?" • Identify a trusted friend or mentor, then send that person a text or email asking, "Can I get your advice when you have a chance?"
#5. Guys should play sports—school... not so much	Trying out new activities I've been curious about	• Set a weekly or monthly goal to try something new, and set reminders (see activity 28) • Write down shorter- and longer-term goals in a visible place so I don't forget about them
	Taking school more seriously and working harder	• Decide on a school-engagement approach (see the "Going Deeper" section after activity 29) • Reach out for help and support from teachers, counselors, trusted friends, or caregivers
#6. Guys shouldn't be like those "other" groups	Not tolerating guys putting down girls and gay people or teasing others with derogatory (anti-gay and anti-female) insults	• Review the tips on taking a stand (see the "Going Deeper" section after activity 34) • Practice and make a commitment to not use these insults myself, and forgive myself for slipups (see the "Going Deeper" section after activity 35)
Other ways to change		

For all of these possible ways to change, there are plenty more skills and resources available online, if you'd like to have even more ways to work on these things. Good luck!

Going Deeper

For all of us, change is a process that takes a lot of work, motivation, and reminders. When you're committed to making a change for yourself, it can be really useful to have a system in place to keep yourself accountable. Without accountability, most of us will forget our goals, and old habits and ways will creep back in. So, here are some tips for putting an accountability system in place:

- Print out the table that's part of activity 41 and keep it in a place where you can see it and be reminded of what you're working on. This visibility will help remind you about possible "ways to change" and new skills, including any that you come up with on your own. (You can download a blank copy of this table to print at http://www .newharbinger.com/49494. See the back of the book for details on this free tool and others associated with this book.)

- Establish weekly reminders of the skills you're working on in your cell phone, on a computer, or using a paper calendar (if you're old-school). For example, I set weekly reminders in Google Calendar that pop up at the beginning of the week. They read something like "Don't forget that you're working on _____" or "Don't forget to talk to _____ about the thing that's bothering you." This may seem overly simple, but quick and brief reminders go a long way in supporting accountability and self-growth.

- Use an actual self-growth tracker to keep yourself accountable. Here's an example. (You can download a blank copy at http://www.newharbinger.com/49494 and then print it.)

Week	Skill(s) I'm Working on This Week	How Did It Go? Any Successes or Slips?
Jan. 23 to 29	1. Getting advice for some dating challenges with my partner 2. Being a better communicator about...	• For #1, I didn't find time and I'm going to try again next week. • For #2, I had a helpful conversation with Brad about the thing he said that bothered me, and I'm feeling better.
Jan. 30 to Feb. 5	1. Getting advice for some dating challenges with my partner 2. Reaching out for help and support with school difficulties in those two harder classes	• For #1, I talked to my friend about worries and relationship issues. He was supportive and gave some helpful advice. • For #2, I didn't have the opportunity and will try again next week.

As you can see, this tracker includes space for writing down the skills you're working on (each week), as well as your progress. I recommend also including your "slips" because none of us can always meet our goals, and sometimes things come up that get in the way of progress. It's useful to note slips, because understanding them may help you more successfully avoid them in the future. For any skill you're working on, keep it on the tracker for as long as feels necessary. Change and skill development take a while, so don't feel bad if you're working on some of these things for months or longer.

The Big Picture: What I'm All About

A lot goes into who you are and what makes you unique, and gender is just one part of that. Over the course of this journey, you've thought more deeply about all sorts of important things, from how the Guy Code works for you to challenging situations you've experienced to your interests and passions to your cultural identities. All of this and much more go into who you are and what you're all about.

At this final stage, you should know yourself even better than when you began this journey. It's time to put all of those different pieces of you together to further solidify the big picture of what makes you unique as a guy and a person.

ACTIVITY 42: "Who Am I?" Profile—Gender and Beyond

We don't often have the chance to fully appreciate ourselves for the different things that make us who we are. You've now spent a good amount of time thinking about yourself as a guy, what works for you and what doesn't, and other important stuff, like your values and cultural identities, all of which provide valuable information for answering these bigger questions:

- Who am I?

- What am I all about?

- How do I want to be?

So, here's an opportunity for a final reflection to bring together the key things you've solidified about yourself over the course of this journey.

For each of the "'stuff I've learned about' questions" in the following table, you'll be prompted to answer with a "fill-in" of your own or by circling "yes," "no," or "kind of." The right-hand column is for your "fill-in" responses, or to write down any additional thoughts you have in response to the questions. You've explored all of these topics already, so I included cross-references to help you locate your earlier reflections, in case doing so might be helpful. (*GD* stands for "Going Deeper" and references a particular "Going Deeper" section in the book.)

"Who Am I?" Profile

"Stuff I've Learned About" Questions	Response Type	Space for Fill-Ins and Additional Thoughts
Who are your most important influences for determining what being a guy means to you?	Fill-in (activity 5)	
Who are the friends and people you trust to be part of your inner circle?	Fill-in (*GD* after activity 10)	
Is it important to have people you can be open with about difficult stuff, including more vulnerable emotions?	Yes/No /Kind of	

"Stuff I've Learned About" Questions	Response Type	Space for Fill-Ins and Additional Thoughts
Is it important to be tough all the time, and to take risks when guys challenge you?	Yes/No /Kind of	
What's your approach to sexual or romantic relationships?	Fill-in (activity 20)	
Do you want to be a more standard alpha male or an agreeable alpha, or is it not important either way?	Fill-in (activity 23)	
Is seeking help important and something that you value?	Yes/No /Kind of	
Are sports important to you?	Yes/No /Kind of	
Is school important to you?	Yes/No /Kind of	
What are your key interests, and what new activities would you like to try?	Fill-in (activity 28)	
Are you okay with guys putting down girls and gay people and using anti-gay and anti-female insults?	Yes/No /Kind of	

"Stuff I've Learned About" Questions	Response Type	Space for Fill-Ins and Additional Thoughts
Are cultural identities important to you? If so, which ones?	Fill-in (*GD* after activity 37)	
What are your most important current and future goals?	Fill-in (activity 29)	
What are some of your core values?	Fill-in (activity 39)	
What ways to change (if any) and skills are you working on?	Fill-in (activity 41)	

Please take a moment to appreciate these things that go into who you are and what you're all about. There you have it. A lot goes into you, and this profile is just scratching the surface. It might be interesting to do this activity annually, as you continue to evolve and get to know yourself and what being a guy means to you even better. (You can download a copy of this activity to print at http://www.newharbinger.com/49494.)

Going Deeper

When you were a kid your world was probably centered on parents and caregivers, but now, as a teenager, peers and establishing greater independence have likely become priorities. Things have changed quite a bit, including your own self-understanding and sense of identity. Your identity will continue to develop for your whole life, but this process is particularly intense during the teen years. So, you're in it!

As you keep moving forward in life as a guy, the activities in this chapter (the tools of which can be downloaded for printing at http://www.newharbinger.com/49494) can continue to be useful:

- **Activity 40: Awakened Masculinity and Me** can be used annually to assess your sense of gender and what being a guy means to you. Your understanding of both will develop and evolve as you get more life experience. In particular, this activity will help you continue to be a critical consumer of the Guy Code by regularly considering what works for you and what doesn't.

- **Activity 41: Self-Growth Strategies and Skills,** along with the self-growth tracker, can be used on a regular basis for developing and maintaining self-growth, and to help you stay on track with your own self-initiated "ways to change" and vision for how you want to be as a guy and a person.

- **Activity 42: "Who Am I?" Profile—Gender and Beyond** is meant to capture your bigger picture, including things related to gender and masculinity, cultural identities, current and future goals, and values. Thus, it can be used as an annual check-in to help you stay connected with who you are and how you're changing. It can also serve as a resource for periodically thinking about values and goals and the stuff that's most important to who you are and how you want to be as a guy and as a person.

As we explored during this journey, societal expectations and Guy Code pressures are no joke. They are powerful forces. It can be easy to get pulled in a direction that isn't true to you, but the tools and resources in this book can support you to keep things real and on your own terms, whatever that means for you and your awakened masculinity.

Moving On

Awesome job making it to the end!

Though you've now completed *The Masculinity Workbook for Teens*, the journey of *who you are* and *how you want to be* is ongoing. Thus, your self-understanding, including what being a guy means to you, will continue to evolve as you live your life and learn more about yourself every day. The self-exploration you just did is a big deal; it's not easy to critically consider and scrutinize something like the Guy Code, which is frequently treated by society as a given, as in "It's just the way all boys and men are, and it's better to not ask questions." Because of assumptions like this, it's uncommon for teen guys to be educated on gender basics and masculinity pressures, and for them to then be invited to decide for themselves, on their own terms, who they are and how they want to be (as guys and as people).

Well, you received that invitation and went for it. So, where do you go from here? Now that you (hopefully) have a clearer sense of who you are as a guy and how you want to be, I hope you continue to go in the direction of being true to the guy and person you are. You've "cracked" the Guy Code, which means you understand, in a way that most guys don't, how society's gender socialization systems function, and the ways that masculinity pressures can be harmful when taken too far. You also hopefully now know, if you didn't before, that there is no "right" approach to being a guy. Masculinities truly represent a spectrum; all it takes is looking around to see evidence of the many different types of guys who are out there, with diverse interests, styles, and ways of being.

As you explored, there are pros and cons to the Guy Code Rules, and you've now deeply considered which ones work for you and which ones don't. Just as society continues to evolve and shift, you will too, as a guy and a person. So, keep your eyes open. I hope you'll stay curious about what being a guy means to you and how you want to be, wherever that may lead.

Travel well,

Chris

Acknowledgments

This undertaking and amazing journey would not have been possible without the considerable support of many wonderful, dedicated, highly skilled, and impassioned people.

To begin, I'd like to thank my wife and life partner, Ashley Emerson, who was an incredible source of support during late nights of writing, took on more of the responsibilities in our home while I wrote this book, and is a true believer in supporting teen guys to "crack the Guy Code." I'm forever grateful, humbled, and awestruck to be the dad of Finn and Fern, who inspire me every day as I continue to learn more about who I am and how I want to be.

I've been very impressed with the professionalism and commitment of the whole New Harbinger team and their dedication to the craft of writing socially impactful books. I was fortunate to land with three special editors, Georgia Kolias, Caleb Beckwith, and James Lainsbury, all of whom were very passionate about and dedicated to partnering on this important project. Their editorial feedback throughout the process was thoughtful, on point, and invaluable, including offering me strategies for writing to teen guys more effectively and making this book as accessible and useful as possible.

My parents, Jisei and Doug, have been a consistent source of support and encouragement as I've found my own way as a guy, figuring out what that means for me in so many different ways. Caroline and Jack have been right there as well and continue to be in big ways.

I've been fortunate to have some key guys in my corner to share laughs with, to climb mountains with, and for when life gets tough. These fellow travelers include Alden Cadwell, Matt Haslett, Andrew Riely, Will Vincent, Geoff Legg, Julian Knox, and Zac Channing.

Two courses in college, in particular, put me on the path to writing this book: "Feminism and Film Theory" with Dr. Laurie Osborne, and "Gender, Race, and the Politics of Difference" with Dr. Cheshire Calhoun. Both of these inspiring and impassioned professors were instrumental in supporting me to think more critically about gender and the Guy Code and what masculinity truly means to me.

In the early days of considering graduate school and career possibilities, Dr. Michael Thompson generously invited me to his house for tea. I've been fortunate to have him as a colleague for the past fifteen years. He is a true leader and visionary in the field of boys' well-being. I am honored that he wrote the foreword for *The Masculinity Workbook for Teens*.

Not many clinical psychologists work in the area of boys' and men's psychology, and I was very fortunate to receive mentoring from Dr. Michael Addis as a doctoral student for six years. I continue to benefit from Michael's expertise, friendship, deep thinking, honesty, and vulnerability. I've also been fortunate to learn from and collaborate with some brilliant, impassioned, and kind scholars and clinicians, including Abbie Goldberg, Esteban Cardemil, Bill Johnson, Matt Englar-Carlson, Andrew Smiler, Ron Levant, Ryon McDermott, Steven Marans, Megan Goslin, Christina Hatgis, Daniel Ellenberg, Jerry Shapiro, Jon Green, Josh Berger, Jon Davies, and Joel Wong—not to mention my other colleagues and friends from the Task Force on Boys in School and the APA's Division 51 (Society for the Psychological Study of Men and Masculinities).

Lastly, I'd like to thank my agent, Kimberley Cameron, a booklover and wonderful advocate.

Appendix A

Sex vs. Gender

Understanding the differences between sex and gender can be challenging. The terms and phrases below are commonly associated with their respective categories. You may be familiar with some, others not so much. The internet or a biology textbook can provide lots of information about all of them, for those who would like to take a deeper look.

Sex	Gender
Male	Boy/man
Female	Girl/woman
Penis	Guy Code
Vagina	Bro Code
Biology	Guys should like sports, etc.
Chemicals/hormones	Girl/Woman Code
Body parts	Girls should like fashion, etc.
XY (male) vs. XX (female) chromosomes	Femininity
Intersex	Masculinity
Estrogen	
Testosterone	

Gender Spectrum Exploration

People can self-identify gender for themselves in many ways that differ from the traditional binary rules and expectations that society has created for boys and men and girls and women. This list of gender spectrum identities is not exhaustive.

Agender: Of, relating to, or being a person who has no gender identity.

Cisgender: Of, relating to, or being a person whose sex type they're born into, also known as the sex assigned at birth, matches their gender identity (including associated behaviors, styles, and interests). For example, if a person is born male due to having XY chromosomes, a penis, and testicles, and that person identifies as a boy or man with regard to their gender identity, then their sex matches their gender identity. (FYI: You don't have to fully or even mostly agree with the Guy Code in order to identify as a boy/man/guy; this is an individual choice and about what feels right for you.)

Gender-fluid: Of, relating to, or being a person whose gender identity is in motion and constantly changing.

Gender nonconforming: Of, relating to, or being a person whose gender expression and appearance don't necessarily conform to societal gender expectations based on the sex assigned to that person at birth.

Genderqueer: Of, relating to, or being a person who doesn't want to be put inside a gender box and doesn't identify with traditional notions of "boy/man," "girl/woman," "masculinity," or "femininity." Some would state that this is a gender category for people who want to be free of society's gender rules and who want to openly define and express themselves with greater freedom and more options. **Gender nonbinary** is similar in meaning. Compared to the traditional gender pronouns of "she/her/hers" and "he/him/his," pronouns that may identify someone as gender nonbinary or genderqueer include "they/them/theirs" and "zie/hir/hirs."

Pangender: Of, relating to, or being a person who is open to all genders as part of their identity and who rejects conforming to the binary perspective.

Transgender: Of, relating to, or being a person whose body they were born into doesn't align with how they view and experience themself as a gendered person. A person may be assigned the female sex type at birth due to their sex organs but may identify as being more masculine. Transgender individuals, also referred to as **trans men** or **trans women**, can pursue different options for expressing themselves, including:

- Social transition, which means living as the gender they identify with and using traditional pronouns or the pronouns of their choice

- Non-hormone-related or nonsurgical changes to appearance, such as clothing, hair, and makeup styles

- Hormonal therapy or surgeries to help their body align with their gender identity

Gottlieb (2019) and Testa, Coolhart, and Peta (2015) are great resources for readers who want to learn more about the gender spectrum and associated identities; full citations for both can be found in the references.

Appendix C

The Gender Boxes Answers

Girl/Woman Code	Guy Code
Sensitive	Tough
Enjoys cooking	Brave and risk taking
More academic/bookish	Athletic
Caregiver/homemaker	Provider/bread winner
Stylish and fashionable	Strong and muscular
Emotionally expressive	Self-reliant
Cooperative and nice	Player and stud
Thin body	Dominant and powerful
More romantic	Emotional control

Appendix D

Guy Code Activities and What You're Into Answers

More for Girls	More for Guys
Fashion or clothes shopping	Playing sports
Cooking or baking	Video games
Art (including pottery, photography, and sculpture)	Mathematics
Choir and singing	Science
School and academics in general	Roughhousing and wrestling
Creative writing	Playing outside
Language arts/English	Outdoor activities (like camping and fishing)
Theater (including acting and dance)	Woodworking or building/fixing stuff
History	
Reading books	
Yoga or fitness classes	
Community service and volunteering	
Sewing, knitting, or other crafts	

Appendix E

A Letter to Caregivers, Parents, and Mentors of Teen Boys

I'm guessing you're reading this letter because you purchased *The Masculinity Workbook for Teens* for a boy in your life whom you care about. If that's the case, way to go! I really wish a guide like this had existed when I was growing up and navigating the topsy-turvy, pressure-filled, and also wondrous years of adolescence. That's why I wrote this book. Being a teenager is no easy thing—for kids of all genders and ages. Adolescence is a developmental stage when so much happens: puberty, dating and sexual exploration, individualizing from caregivers, identity and gender development, middle school and high school, and so much more.

In addition to the standard challenges that all adolescents face, teen boys in particular receive constant pressure to be "a certain way" as guys due to the Guy Code and resulting masculinity pressures, as you likely know. The Guy Code is the set of rules that society—and consequently many boys, adults, and other people—expects teen guys, like the ones you know, to follow in order to be accepted. Whether you agree with the rules or not, you're likely familiar with them. (Any come to mind as you read this?) They include things like the pressure to be tough, hide emotions, be in control, play sports, and prove oneself sexually with girls. Guys start receiving masculinity teachings about these rules and how they should be early in childhood, with one common teaching being "Big boys don't cry." Boys let us know they're absorbing these messages as "No girls allowed" games become a thing, sometimes as early as kindergarten, and by beginning to tease boys who don't adequately conform to such norms.

In spite of receiving clear and unmistakable messages from society about how they should be, boys *often* aren't taught much about how gender works and what exactly the Guy Code is. Also, most guys aren't frequently encouraged to find their own way, whether that ultimately leads them in the direction of the Guy Code or somewhere else. And that's exactly what *The Masculinity Workbook for Teens* is all about: providing teen boys with a clear, experiential, and nonprescriptive resource on what gender is and how the Guy Code works, and, most importantly, the encouragement to establish for themselves how they want to be as guys and as people. As I state throughout, my only agenda is educating teen guys about gender and the Guy Code, so they'll be better positioned to make *their own* decisions about who they are and how they want to be.

So, let me tell you a little bit about *The Masculinity Workbook for Teens* and what to expect. The first two chapters are focused on gender basics, including background information on what gender is, the Guy Code, and key terms that are important for all of us to know. The text supports readers as they assess their own knowledge about gender and the Guy Code and start to explore how they've been socialized and who has been influential in teaching them about masculinity and what it means to be a guy. Part 2 focuses on the six key rules that boys are pressured to follow throughout childhood and adolescence, such as the importance of toughness, of being a player, and of hiding emotions. While awareness building is a goal of part 2, the primary objective is for boys to reflect on and explore how each of the Guy Code Rules has worked for them. Part 3 includes a chapter on cultural exploration to help readers better understand how their cultural identities have influenced them with regard to gender (and in general). The workbook concludes with a chapter that helps readers further solidify what they've learned about themselves, as guys and as people, along with skill builders for teen boys who want to make some changes.

While *The Masculinity Workbook for Teens* is written in a way so teen guys can navigate the information on their own, it includes lots of important information about gender and masculinity pressures that parents, caregivers, and mentors will benefit from. An additional way to utilize the workbook, if the teen boy you got this for *is willing*, is to discuss the content of each chapter with him and share your own experiences with Guy Code pressures when you were younger. All boys stand to benefit from a caring adult taking the time to talk to them about masculinity pressures, including their perspective on the pros and cons of these different pressures, even if these conversations get awkward at times. These types of discussions aren't easy, but they're important and don't happen enough. *The Masculinity Workbook for Teens* includes a number of structural elements to make these types of conversations easier and more fruitful, including "Stop and Think" questions, "Research Moments," and "Words of Guys" sections, as well as activities throughout that can be completed individually (or jointly) and then discussed.

So, that's a bit of what to expect. It's awesome that you're sharing this book with a teen boy who's important to you. I'm always happy to hear from readers and the adults in their lives, and you can contact me through my website, http:// chrisreigeluth.com, with questions or comments. Hopefully, by providing boys with a greater understanding of the masculinity pressures they face, and the space and reassurance they need to freely explore and express who they are and how they want to be, we can better support them to live lives of greater happiness and fulfillment.

Take care, and many thanks,

Chris Reigeluth

A Letter to Therapists, School Counselors, Coaches, Group Leaders, Wellness Instructors, and Others Who Support Boys

I'm guessing you're reading this letter because you already do work with boys, or have an interest in doing so. That's awesome and is very needed! You might be wondering, *So, what are some ways that* The Masculinity Workbook for Teens *might be a fit for my work with boys?* Well, whether you work with individuals or with groups, this book could be quite a useful resource if you are, or want to be, someone who encourages boys to think more deeply about healthy gender identity and what being a guy means to them.

I really wish a guide like this had existed when I was growing up and navigating the topsy-turvy, pressure-filled, and also wondrous years of adolescence. That's why I wrote this book. Being a teenager is no easy thing—for kids of all genders and ages. Adolescence is a developmental stage when so much happens: puberty, dating and sexual exploration, individualizing from caregivers, identity and gender development, middle school and high school, and so much more.

In addition to the standard challenges that all adolescents face, teen boys in particular receive constant pressure to be "a certain way" as guys due to the Guy Code and resulting masculinity pressures, as you know. The Guy Code is the set of rules that society—and consequently many boys, adults, and other people—expects teen guys, like the ones you know, to follow in order to be accepted. The rules include things like pressure to be tough, hide emotions, be in control, play sports, and prove oneself sexually with girls. Guys start receiving masculinity messages about these rules and how they should be early in childhood, with one common teaching being "Big boys don't cry." Some boys let us know they're absorbing these messages as "No girls allowed" games become a thing, sometimes as early as kindergarten, and by teasing boys who don't adequately conform to such norms.

In spite of receiving clear and unmistakable messages from society about how they should be, boys *often* aren't taught much about how gender works and what exactly the Guy Code is. Also, most guys aren't frequently encouraged to find their own way, whether that ultimately leads them in the direction of the Guy Code or somewhere else. And that's exactly what *The Masculinity Workbook for Teens* is all about: providing teen boys with a clear, experiential, and nonprescriptive resource on what gender is and how the Guy Code works, and, most importantly, the encouragement to establish for themselves how they want to be as guys and as people. As I state throughout, my only agenda is educating teen guys about gender and the Guy Code, so they'll be better positioned to make *their own* decisions about who they are and how they want to be.

So, let me tell you a little bit about *The Masculinity Workbook for Teens* and what to expect. The first two chapters are focused on gender basics, including background information on what gender is, the Guy Code, and key terms that are important for all of us to know. The text supports readers as they assess their own knowledge about gender and the Guy Code and start to explore how they've been socialized and who has been influential in teaching them about masculinity and what it means to be a guy. Part 2 focuses on the six key rules that boys are pressured to follow throughout childhood and adolescence, such as the importance of toughness, of being a player, and of hiding emotions. While awareness building is a goal of part 2, the primary objective is for boys to reflect on and explore how each of the Guy Code Rules has worked for them. Part 3 includes a chapter on cultural exploration to help readers better understand how their cultural identities have influenced them with regard to gender (and in general). The workbook concludes with a chapter for readers to further solidify what they've learned about themselves, as guys and as people, along with skill builders for teen boys who want to make some changes.

For leaders of groups for boys (or those aspiring to lead), *The Masculinity Workbook for Teens* can serve a variety of functions, from operating as your primary group curriculum to supplementing a curriculum already in place. Depending on how long your group will run, the content of each of the nine chapters can be covered as a single session or be broken up over multiple sessions. Prior to each session or group meeting, assign the chapter being covered, along with the accompanying activities. Then, in reviewing and completing each chapter for yourself, decide what content to integrate into your group plan.

Leaders with more time might cover most of the content in the workbook by presenting key concepts and then facilitating group discussions (or smaller breakout groups) that include participants sharing their responses to the different activities. Each chapter is broken into three to five sections that introduce a new concept and include an experiential activity about that concept; and each section ends with a brief "going deeper" exercise. Additionally, each chapter includes a few common features that lend themselves well to group exploration:

- **Words of Guys:** These include short quotes from real teen boys of all different backgrounds—the real experts—reflecting on their experiences with the Guy Code and masculinity pressures.

- **Stop and Think:** These provide questions for readers to think about more deeply for themselves.

- **Research Moments:** These offer scientific findings related to research on boys, men, and gender.

- **What's Your Take?** Only included in part 2, these focus on a specific Guy Code Rule and end with a final written reflection through which readers can further evaluate the pros and cons of the rule, including what's worked for them and what hasn't.

Leaders with less time can still utilize the above illustrative plan; they will just need to be more selective with the content they cover. Of course, all group leaders should provide space for participants to ask questions and provide input on the content that feels most important to them to explore.

For people working with boys individually, such as therapists and life coaches, you can use *The Masculinity Workbook for Teens* following the above recommended approach. You can also use it more selectively based on the presenting issues:

- Teen boys struggling with general identity-based uncertainty or stress will benefit from going through the full workbook as a way of getting to know themselves better, including what being a guy means to them, and then processing their reflections with you.

- Teen boys with a specific challenge, such as emotional restriction or aggression, will benefit from exploring the introductory chapters (and accompanying activities) in their sessions with you as a way to understand how masculinity pressures may be influencing them and their behaviors. You can then select specific chapters based on the issue (for example, chapter 2 for a teen guy struggling with emotional restriction, and chapter 5 for one experiencing difficulties with aggression or seeking help). You should encourage them to read the rest of the workbook on their own and to bring up any content that seems helpful in sessions with you.

- Boys questioning their gender identity, or feeling like traditional masculinity approaches are not a great fit for them, can use the workbook to clarify what specific aspects of the Guy Code aren't working for them while more clearly establishing who they are and how they want to be.

So, those are some tips and ideas for using *The Masculinity Workbook for Teens* with groups or individuals in a clinical or coaching setting. I'm always happy to hear from readers and the people supporting boys. You can contact me through my website, http://chrisreigeluth.com. I'm also available for consultation for individuals interested in exploring further the different ways to use the workbook, and for institutions, such as schools, looking to develop a healthy gender curriculum for boys, along with other students, as part of a wellness or social emotional learning (SEL) program.

Hopefully, by providing boys with a greater understanding of the masculinity pressures they face, and the space and reassurance they need to freely explore and express who they are and how they want to be, we can better support them to live lives of greater happiness and fulfillment.

Take care, and many thanks,

Chris Reigeluth

References

Arnett, J. J. 2018. *Adolescence and Emerging Adulthood: A Cultural Approach*. 6th ed. Hoboken, NJ: Pearson.

Ashmore, R. D., F. K. Del Boca, and M. Beebe. 2002. "'Alkie,' 'Frat Brother,' and 'Jock': Perceived Types of College Students and Stereotypes About Drinking." *Journal of Applied Social Psychology* 32: 885–907.

Bandura, A. 1977. *Social Learning Theory*. Englewood Cliffs, NJ: Prentice-Hall.

Bartholow, B. D., B. J. Bushman, and M. A. Sestir. 2006. "Chronic Violent Video Game Exposure and Desensitization to Violence: Behavioral and Event-Related Brain Potential Data." *Journal of Experimental Social Psychology* 42: 532–39.

Brackett, M. A., S. E. Rivers, and P. Salovey. 2011. "Emotional Intelligence: Implications for Personal, Social, Academic, and Workplace Success." *Social and Personality Psychology Compass* 5: 88–103.

Chu, J. Y. 2014. *When Boys Become Boys: Development, Relationships, and Masculinity*. New York: New York University Press.

Connell, R. W. 2005. *Masculinities*. 2nd ed. Berkeley: University of California Press.

Connett, W. 2021. "10 Top Women CEOs." Investopedia. Updated March 5. https://www.investopedia.com/news/top-women-ceos.

Courtenay, W. 2011. *Dying to Be Men: Psychosocial, Environmental, and Biobehavioral Directions in Promoting the Health of Men and Boys*. New York: Routledge.

Crenshaw, K. 1991. "Mapping the Margins: Intersectionality, Identity Politics, and Violence Against Women of Color." *Stanford Law Review* 43: 1241–99.

DeBate, R. D., A. Gatto, and G. Rafal. 2018. "The Effects of Stigma on Determinants of Mental Health Help-Seeking Behaviors Among Male College Students: An Application of the Information-Motivation-Behavioral Skills Model." *American Journal of Men's Health* 12: 1286–96.

Eichstadt, M., J. Luzier, D. Cho, and C. Weisenmuller. 2020. "Eating Disorders in Male Athletes." *Sports Health: A Multidisciplinary Approach* 12: 327–33.

Ferguson, R. F. 2016. *Aiming Higher Together: Strategizing Better Educational Outcomes for Boys and Young Men of Color*. Research Report. Urban Institute. https://www.urban

.org/research/publication/aiming-higher-together-strategizing-better-educational
-outcomes-boys-and-young-men-color/view/full_report.

Frosh, S., A. Phoenix, and R. Pattman. 2002. *Young Masculinities: Understanding Boys in Contemporary Society*. New York: Palgrave.

Gilmore, D. D. 1990. *Manhood in the Making: Cultural Concepts of Masculinity*. New Haven, CT: Yale University Press.

Gottlieb, I. 2019. *Seeing Gender: An Illustrated Guide to Identity and Expression*. San Francisco: Chronicle Books.

Hays, P. A. 2016. *Addressing Cultural Complexities in Practice: Assessment, Diagnosis, and Therapy*. 3rd ed. Washington, DC: American Psychological Association.

Howard, G. S. 1991. "Cultural Tales: A Narrative Approach to Thinking, Cross-Cultural Psychology, and Psychotherapy." *American Psychologist* 46: 187–97.

Hunter, A. G., and J. E. Davis. 1992. "Constructing Gender: An Exploration of Afro-American Men's Conceptualization of Manhood." *Gender and Society* 6: 464–79.

Institute of Education Sciences. 2021. *Report on the Condition of Education 2021*. Washington, DC: US Department of Education. https://nces.ed.gov/pubs2021 /2021144.pdf.

Iwamoto, D. K., and A. Kaya. 2016. "Asian American Men." In *APA Handbook of Men and Masculinities*, edited by Y. J. Wong and S. R. Wester. Washington, DC: American Psychological Association.

Keith, T. 2021. *The Bro Code: The Fallout of Raising Boys to Objectify and Subordinate Women*. New York: Routledge.

Kennedy-Moore, E., and J. C. Watson. 2001. "How and When Does Emotional Expression Help?" *Review of General Psychology* 5: 187–212.

Kimmel, M. 2008. *Guyland: The Perilous World Where Boys Become Men*. New York: HarperCollins.

Kimmel, M. 2016. *The Gendered Society*. 6th ed. New York: Oxford University Press.

Kimmel, M. S., and A. L. Ferber (Eds.). 2017. *Privilege: A Reader*. 4th ed. New York: Routledge.

Kindlon, D., and M. Thompson. 1999. *Raising Cain: Protecting the Emotional Life of Boys*. New York: Ballantine Books.

Kivel, P. 1992. *Men's Work: How to Stop the Violence That Tears Our Lives Apart*. New York: Ballantine Books.

Levant, R. F., B. K. Rogers, B. Cruickshank, T. J. Rankin, B. A. Kurtz, C. M. Rummell, C. M. Williams, and A. J. Colbow. 2012. "Exploratory Factor Analysis and Construct Validity of the Male Role Norms Inventory-Adolescent-Revised (MRNI-A-r)." *Psychology of Men and Masculinity* 13: 354–66.

Liang, C. T. H., G. H. Rocchino, M. H. C. Gutekunst, and A. Smithson. 2019. "Conformity to Masculinity Ideology, a Predictor of Academic-Related Attitudes and Behaviors." *Psychology in the Schools* 56: 1583–95.

Mahalik, J. R., E. B. Morray, A. Coonerty-Femiano, L. H. Ludlow, S. M. Slattery, and A. Smiler. 2005. "Development of the Conformity to Feminine Norms Inventory." *Sex Roles* 52: 417–35.

Majors, R., and J. M. Billson. 1993. *Cool Pose: The Dilemmas of Black Manhood in America*. New York: Touchstone Books/Simon & Schuster.

Martin, C. L., D. N. Ruble, and J. Szkrybalo. 2002. "Cognitive Theories of Early Gender Development." *Psychological Bulletin* 128: 903–33.

Messner, M. A. 1995. *Power at Play: Sports and the Problem of Masculinity*. Boston: Beacon Press.

Mora, R. 2012. "'Do It for All Your Pubic Hairs!': Latino Boys, Masculinity, and Puberty." *Gender and Society* 26: 433–60.

Oransky, M., and C. Fisher. 2009. "The Development and Validation of the Meanings of Adolescent Masculinity Scale." *Psychology of Men and Masculinity* 10: 57–72.

Oransky, M., and J. Marecek. 2009. "'I'm Not Going to Be a Girl': Masculinity and Emotions in Boys' Friendships and Peer Groups." *Journal of Adolescent Research* 24: 218–41.

Orenstein, P. 2020. *Boys and Sex: Young Men on Hookups, Love, Porn, Consent, and Navigating the New Masculinity*. New York: HarperCollins.

Owens, J. 2016. "Early Childhood Behavior Problems and the Gender Gap in Educational Attainment in the United States." *Sociology of Education* 89: 236–58.

Pollack, W. 1998. *Real Boys: Rescuing Our Sons from the Myths of Boyhood*. New York: Owl Books.

Reigeluth, C. S. in press. "Gender Socialization of Boys and (Un)Intended Consequences." In *The Encyclopedia of Child and Adolescent Health*, edited by B. Halpern-Felsher. Amsterdam: Elsevier.

Reigeluth, C. S., and M. E. Addis. 2016. "Adolescent Boys' Experiences with Policing of Masculinity: Forms, Functions, and Consequences." *Psychology of Men and Masculinity* 17: 74–83.

Reigeluth, C. S., and M. E. Addis. 2021. "Policing of Masculinity Scale (POMS) and Pressures Boys Experience to Prove and Defend Their 'Manhood.'" *Psychology of Men and Masculinities* 22: 306–20.

Rouse, L. M. 2016. "American Indians, Alaskan Natives, and the Psychology of Men and Masculinity." In *APA Handbook of Men and Masculinities*, edited by Y. J. Wong and S. R. Wester. Washington, DC: American Psychological Association.

Sapolsky, R. M. 1997. *The Trouble with Testosterone: And Other Essays on the Biology of the Human Predicament*. New York: Simon & Schuster.

Scott, K. 2016. "Ethical Porn—Does It Exist and Who Makes It?" ABC News (Australian Broadcasting Corporation). Updated December 21. https://www.abc.net.au/news /2016-12-21/ethical-porn-does-it-exist-and-where-do-you-find-it/8091266#:~:text=%22 But%20porn%20can%20be%20better,rather%20how%20it%20is%20used.&text=Paying %20for%20porn%20is%20also,ethical%20production%2C%20Dr%20Watson%20says.

Siebel Newsom, J. (Director). 2015. *The Mask You Live In*. Film. The Representation Project. https://therepproject.org/films/the-mask-you-live-in.

Shollenberger, T. L. 2015. "Racial Disparities in School Suspension and Subsequent Outcomes: Evidence from the National Longitudinal Survey of Youth." In *Closing the School Discipline Gap: Equitable Remedies for Excessive Exclusion*, edited by D. J. Losen. New York: Teachers College Press.

Smiler, A. 2019. *Is Masculinity Toxic? A Primer for the 21st Century*. London: Thames and Hudson.

Smiler, A. P. 2006. "Living the Image: A Quantitative Approach to Delineating Masculinities." *Sex Roles: A Journal of Research* 55: 621–32.

Smiler, A. P. 2013. *Challenging Casanova: Beyond the Stereotype of the Promiscuous Young Male*. San Francisco: Josey-Bass.

Smiler, A. P. 2016. *Dating and Sex: A Guide for the 21st Century Teen Boy*. Washington, DC: Magination Press.

Solnit, R. 2008. "Men Explain Things to Me; Facts Didn't Get in Their Way." Common Dreams. April 13. https://www.commondreams.org/views/2008/04/13/men-explain -things-me-facts-didnt-get-their-way.

Steinberg, L. 2014. *Age of Opportunity: Lessons from the New Science of Adolescence*. Boston: Houghton Mifflin Harcourt.

Testa, R. J., D. Coolhart, and J. Peta. 2015. *The Gender Quest Workbook: A Guide for Teens and Young Adults Exploring Gender Identity*. Oakland, CA: Instant Help Books.

Way, N. 2011. *Deep Secrets: Boys' Friendships and the Crisis of Connection*. Cambridge, MA: Harvard University Press.

Way, N., J. Cressen, S. Bodian, J. Preston, J. Nelson, and D. Hughes. 2014. "'It Might Be Nice to Be a Girl… Then You Wouldn't Have to Be Emotionless: Boys' Resistance to Norms of Masculinity During Adolescence." *Psychology of Men and Masculinity* 15: 241–52.

Wright, P. J., B. Paul, and D. Herbenick. 2021. "Preliminary Insights from a U.S. Probability Sample on Adolescents' Pornography Exposure, Media Psychology, and Sexual Aggression." *Journal of Health Communication* 26: 39–46.

Vandello, J. A., J. K. Bosson, D. Cohen, R. M. Burnaford, and J. R. Weaver. 2008. "Precarious Manhood." *Journal of Personality and Social Psychology* 95: 1325–39.

Christopher S. Reigeluth, PhD, is assistant professor in the division of clinical psychology at Oregon Health & Science University, and past fellow at the Yale Child Study Center. He is a child and adolescent psychologist who is passionate about the well-being of boys and men and greater gender awareness for all people. Chris loves the outdoors, and lives in Portland, Oregon with his wife, Ashley, and their children, Finn and Fern.

Foreword writer **Michael G. Thompson, PhD**, is a clinical psychologist, author, and school consultant. He is author or coauthor of ten books, including the *New York Times* bestseller, *Raising Cain*.

More Instant Help Books for Teens

An Imprint of New Harbinger Publications

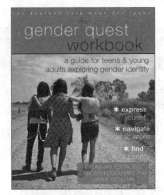

THE ANGER MANAGEMENT WORKBOOK FOR TEEN BOYS

CBT Skills to Defuse Triggers, Manage Difficult Emotions, and Resolve Issues Peacefully

978-1684039074 / US $18.95

THE GENDER QUEST WORKBOOK

A Guide for Teens and Young Adults Exploring Gender Identity

978-1626252974 / US $17.95

YOUR LIFE, YOUR WAY

Acceptance and Commitment Therapy Skills to Help Teens Manage Emotions and Build Resilience

978-1684034659 / US $17.95

OVERCOMING SUICIDAL THOUGHTS FOR TEENS

CBT Activities to Reduce Pain, Increase Hope, and Build Meaningful Connections

978-1684039975 / US $18.95

THE SOCIALLY CONFIDENT TEEN

An Attachment Theory Workbook to Help You Feel Good about Yourself and Connect with Others

978-1684038725 / US $18.95

THE SELF-ESTEEM WORKBOOK FOR TEENS, SECOND EDITION

Activities to Help You Build Confidence and Achieve Your Goals

978-1648480003 / US $18.95

newharbingerpublications

1-800-748-6273 / newharbinger.com

(VISA, MC, AMEX / prices subject to change without notice)

Follow Us

Don't miss out on new books from New Harbinger.
Subscribe to our email list at **newharbinger.com/subscribe**

Did you know there are **free tools** you can download for this book?

Free tools are things like **worksheets**, **guided meditation exercises**, and **more** that will help you get the most out of your book.

You can download free tools for this book— whether you bought or borrowed it, in any format, from any source—from the New Harbinger website. All you need is a NewHarbinger.com account. Just use the URL provided in this book to view the free tools that are available for it. Then, click on the "download" button for the free tool you want, and follow the prompts that appear to log in to your NewHarbinger.com account and download the material.

You can also save the free tools for this book to your **Free Tools Library** so you can access them again anytime, just by logging in to your account! Just look for this button on the book's free tools page. ➔ **+ Save this to my free tools library**

If you need help accessing or downloading free tools, visit **newharbinger.com/faq** or contact us at **customerservice@newharbinger.com**.